grace
& demion

grace & demion

A Fable for Victims of Biblical Intolerance

Mel White

Wideness Press
Long Beach CA

Published in 2014 by Lethe Press, Inc.

Re-released 2017 by Wideness Press, Long Beach CA

melwhite.org   GraceandDemion@gmail.com

These stories are works of fiction. Names, characters, places, and incidents are products of the author's imagination or are used fictitiously.

Cover and Interior design: David Kerley

Interior design images ©iStock.com/DrPAS

Cover and "Confession" illustrations by Charles Hefling

ISBN-13: 978-1976481338

ISBN-10: 1976481333

Library of Congress Cataloging-in-Publication Data
for large format 1st edition

White, Mel, 1940- author.
 Grace & Demion : a fable for victims of biblical intolerance / Mel White.
   pages cm

    "Underwritten by an Author Grant from Peter Drake's Coil Foundation."

    ISBN 978-1-59021-596-8 -- ISBN 1-59021-596-6

    1. Homosexuality--Religious aspects--Fiction. 2. Christian fiction. I. Title.
        PS3573.H474446G73 2014
        813'.54--dc23
                            2014036905

ADVANCE PRAISE FOR GRACE & DEMION

Mel's book is lovely, touching. I was moved by it. It reminds me in tone and purity of The Little Prince. Grace and Demion could become a classic.

Frank Schaeffer, author, **Why I Am an Atheist Who Believes in God**

This intriguing fable would make an excellent animated movie or video — go for it!

Tony Campolo, Ph.D., popular speaker, sociologist, author

I was reminded of The Shack. A playful way to deal with a serious issue.

The Rev. Mendle Adams, clergyman. seminary professor

Brave and innovative. Amazing new way to bring hope to GLBTQ people rejected by family and friends because of those miserable Bible passages used to condemn them.

The Rev. Ken Martin, MCC Elder

Delightful. Covers all the bases with a light touch. I found my eyes filling as I read the section on the Tower. Brings to mind the Screwtape Letters especially when Demion is coached to whisper to God's queer children that they need to change.

Babs Conant, Ph.D., long-time lesbian activist and supporter

This story is heart-wrenching and healing. The book took on an Aesop's fable imagery for me at the end.

Cindi Love, Ed.D., former Executive Director, Soulforce

Enchanting. Reminds me of the tender, magical landscape of a Richard Bach novel.

Lee Ellis, actor, singer-songwriter and composer

...Endorsements continued at back of book

Someday you will be old enough to start reading fairy tales again.

~ C. S. Lewis

Contents

(A Confession)

During my teenage years I was told that my homosexuality was "from the devil" and that being Gay would send me "straight to hell." Sixty-one years later well-meaning Christians still misuse the Bible to warn LGBTQ teenagers that their sexual orientation is "from the devil" and that accepting themselves as they are will send them "straight to hell."

If those same well-meaning Christians are so determined to misuse heaven and hell, angels and demons to scare LGBTQ teenagers into believing that God won't love them unless they "change," I'm equally determined to use heaven and hell, **Grace and Demion** to show my sisters and brothers that God has created them and loves them exactly as they are.

Sixty-one years have passed since I first met Grace, the guardian angel of God's LGBTQ creations and Demion, her hunky little adversary. I was a thirteen-year-old Boy Scout experiencing my first crush on another Boy Scout when they suddenly appeared in my life.

I have to admit that six decades later there are still times I'm hassled by Demion. At the same time, Grace has never failed me. Every day she reminds me that as an out gay man I am loved unconditionally by my Creator and just knowing that has made all the difference.

Mel White
June, 2014

 Introductions

HEAVEN

In heaven there is no class system. Gabriel and the other Named Ones may have special tasks. Spirit Guides and Guardians like Grace may be away temporarily on assignment but without exception every citizen of heaven is equal. Newly liberated souls arriving daily have no trouble fitting in. Even God hangs out.

GRACE

Grace is being trained for duty. On the surface she has almost no advantages, no special skills, and no special beauty. She is timid, smaller than most angels with a rather cute but common face, unruly hair, a total disinterest in playing the harp, and endless questions; but there is something endearing about Grace, something fearless, something that makes you love and trust her in spite of her apparent inadequacies.

HELL

In hell there are no Vice Presidents. Satan is boss. He loves to give himself new titles: Father of Lies, Ruler of Darkness, Prince of the Underworld. Archdemons rank first in hell's hierarchy, then Demons First and Second Class, Fiends, Sprites, Imps and all the devils without titles like Demion who will not be titled until he has terrorized a co-worker in hell or better yet deceived a person on earth.

DEMION

Demion is still a demon in training but he has advantages (that he is only beginning to discover): devilish good looks, absolutely no moral values, a mean spirit and a conscience made in hell. He is taller than most other demons with "flashing brown eyes, spiky hair, quick wits, a tightly muscled body, and the natural, inborn instincts of a bully."

"In the Beginning..."

In the beginning, my beginning, God created that little Gay baby who was born and given my name seventy-four years ago. Now I know for certain that all LGBTQ Children are also the handiwork of our loving Creator, but for more than forty painful years, I had trouble believing it.

Fortunately, from my earliest childhood there were memories that gave me hope, memories I could not quite recall, haunting memories of another time and place, urgent memories that called out to me in the night, echoes of voices and song, moving shadows like dreams that rush away with the morning light leaving only scattered fragments, pieces of a puzzle that I could not put together.

Then, unexpectedly, after years of guilt and self-hatred, after endless "ex-gay" therapy sessions, electric-shock and even exorcism, after slashing at my wrists and longing for death, I suddenly remembered it all. The pieces of the dream fell into place at last and I can tell you exactly when and where it happened.

I was lying on the bed in our rented cottage in Laguna Beach. In the silence, I could hear the surf pounding against the rocks and the occasional bark of a sea lion on seal rock. Gary, my partner for thirty plus years had fallen asleep beside me. The room was completely dark and silent. At the very moment I rolled over and cuddled up against him, those memories, more than half-a-century old, finally came back to me.

I was a thirteen-year-old Boy Scout camping in an ancient grove of redwood trees in the hills above Santa Cruz, California. My tent mate was sleeping soundly while I lay beside him wide awake embarrassed and confused by what I was feeling. Earlier that evening we had dressed in loin clothes like those worn by Native American youth who once inhabited those hills overlooking the blue Pacific. I was painting my tent mate's bare chest with the bright colors of the

"Coastal People" when my body betrayed me. The night was dark. No one seemed to notice.

Later as I watched him sleeping beside me it happened again. I wanted to touch him, to climb into his sleeping bag and hold him. I was terrified by these unwanted feelings. I didn't know then that I was a gay man, that my feelings were right and natural. I didn't even know what it meant to be gay let alone why my body was suddenly responding on its own. I was lying there praying that God would take away those feelings when I heard the distant cry of a thirsty coyote, a common sound in those rolling hills especially during the dry summer months.

It took more than fifty years to discover it wasn't a coyote that howled that night. It was a tough little soul thief named Demion who had been tackled and pinned to the ground just outside my tent by Grace, the guardian angel of God's LGBTQ children. Demion was equipped by Satan himself to steal my soul. God had prepared Grace to keep that from happening.

Now I realize that Grace and Demion have been my constant companions since that night when I was just thirteen. During a recent uneasy truce between them, I asked Grace about her training in heaven. What message did she have for me from my Creator? And I asked Demion what he learned in hell to keep me from hearing it. This is what they told me.

Another Gay Child is Born
(June 26, 1940)

"Sing, angel choirs! Play, angel bands! Quick, angel color guards raise another lavender flag over the parapets of heaven. Come quickly, saints and martyrs. Gather around to cheer, and weep, and wonder why every so often God orders another Queer Child to be born."

The Archangel Gabriel

God was missing again and all the heavenly host were beginning to panic. Angels and archangels, saints and martyrs, even the tiny cherubs were searching high and low for their Creator. In fact, it was a rather courageous cherub who fluttered on her tiny wings past the "Do Not Disturb" sign into the private offices of the Archangel Gabriel where she hovered above him just long enough to blurt out the news.

"God has disappeared," she squealed in genuine alarm. "What shall we do?"

Gabriel smiled to himself. Without looking up at the terrified cherub, he blotted his parchment and wiped extra ink off his quill.

"Tell your sisters and brothers not to worry," the Archangel said calmly. "I know exactly where to find our Friend."

The cherub bowed low as Gabriel spoke one of God's other names, but then darted back out the window, forgetting heavenly protocol, excited to share the hopeful news.

Gabriel hurried from the room, still smiling. He knew exactly where the Creator would be. And why not? From almost the beginning of time, Gabriel had been one of the Creator's closest friends and co-workers, rushing about the universe on errands at God's command. It was Gabriel who promised Hagar that her children, too, would become a great nation. Gabriel who warned Lot and his daughters to flee from Sodom; Gabriel who stopped the hand of Abraham before he sacrificed his young son, Isaac; Gabriel who announced to an unwed teenage mother that she would conceive, bring forth a child, and name him Jesus; and nine months later the same Gabriel who scared sleeping shepherds and their sheep with a loud hallelujah chorus in the night.

God loves all children and takes a special interest in their birth. Often the Creator Himself stands by to witness the children being born. Gabriel knew that he would find God there, smiling down at the mothers of the world who are God's co-creators, groaning with their pain, feeling their terror, and finally celebrating their relief when nine months of discomfort, nausea, and frightening fantasies finally finish with a newborn child in their arms.

There is a light at the center of heaven that is so bright that no one dares to enter it but the Creator. It is the birthing light. And in that light I, too, was born. Sadly for my first forty years of life I wasn't sure that God had created me Gay or that God loved me exactly as I had been created. Then, cuddled up against Gary in our cottage in Laguna Beach, I relived it all, in a dream, as it had been, from the beginning.

For nine months I had floated safely suspended inside my mother in her sensuous, silken sack. Then, without warning, the water that had cradled me so gently just drained away and I began the final terrifying plunge from that other world into this. At the end of the long, slippery tunnel there were voices that I had never heard before, my mother groaning in pain, a nurse whispering, "Push harder, Mrs. White," the doctor saying quietly, "Here he comes."

But even with all those distracting new sounds rushing up at me, I could still hear the friendly, familiar voice of the Archangel Gabriel growing ever more distant as I slid precariously toward the light. When he knew my time had come, Gabriel rushed down the golden streets of heaven shouting at the top of his voice.

"Sing, angel choirs! Play, angel bands! Quick, angel color guards raise another lavender flag over the parapets of heaven. Come quickly, saints and martyrs. Gather around to cheer, and weep, and wonder why every so often God orders another Gay Child to be born."

With Gabriel, himself, crying out the news, the sky above Stanford Memorial Hospital in Palo Alto, California, filled with angels and archangels, cherubim and seraphim, saints and martyrs. In fact, my father, speeding towards the hospital along Bay Shore Highway, still remembers turning on his headlights in the middle of the day and staring in amazement at the shimmering cloud that suddenly appeared between the earth and the sun.

With everyone focused on my mother, no one in the hospital room even noticed the little angels hovering above my mother's head. But I saw them and at night, when Gary is sleeping and the world is almost silent, I can almost see them still.

"Why do you think God loves them so?" asked a cherub, hovering over the scene of my birth like a hummingbird above a field of flowers.

"Why not?" a seraph replied indignantly. "God loves everyone God makes!"

Suddenly, above the noisy, festive scene, the Creator and Sustainer of the Universe appeared. For a moment God just stared silently into that little hospital room where another Gay Child had just been born. During the silence, the company of saints and angels that was gathering to worship the Creator grew so large that their line stretched far beyond the horizon to infinity.

"You ask why another Gay Child is born today?" the Divine asked and billions of saints and angels nodded their heads and looked perplexed. "Because they give me joy." For a moment God paused. "And it's not just the Gay ones," God added. "The Lesbians, the Bis, the Transgender — I rejoice in all my Queer Children."

"But why do you call them Queer?" whispered a very brave angel. "Isn't that what the other side calls them?"

For a moment God was silent remembering how the word "Queer" had been misused over the centuries to condemn anyone who was different from the norm. But to the Creator being different was a gift, another way of saying "unique," "unconventional," "set apart."

"Queer may be an ugly word," God continued, "especially when Satan and his friends use it as a curse. In fact to be Queer, to be different from the norm is a blessing, a gift I have given them, a view of life that is unique, powerful enough to bring hope and healing to my troubled world."

Then after another long moment of silence, the Creator smiled and spoke again. "Besides, my Queer Children stir things up and God knows that the world needs an occasional stir."

Looking down on that wrinkled, pink, satisfied child nursing at my mother's breast our Creator laughed with delight and for a long time God's laughter boomed across the heavens until all the angels, even the grumpy ones, were laughing.

At that very same moment, in the deepest, darkest, dreariest pit of hell, directly over the fiery furnace, Satan himself heard the Creator's laughter. "Another Queer child is born," the Prince of Darkness growled happily to his Archdemon. "Will God never learn? They may have the power to bring hope and healing to the world but not after we're finished with them."

And with those words, their fiendish cackle threatened to drown out the Creator's loving laughter.

"If God is willing to risk their fresh little souls," Satan sneered, "we are more than happy to take the challenge."

The sycophant Archdemon Fury was still laughing when the Devil bellowed, "Get on with it! We have another Queer soul to maim. There is no time to lose!"

Now, looking back over all those more than forty years of fear and trembling, it is no wonder that I could barely recall God's loving laughter, for the maternity ward also echoed with the fiendish sounds of hell. God had seemed so close inside my mother's womb, but it was hard to even remember my Creator's smile with the doctor grabbing me by the heels, lifting me above the gurney, and slapping my little pink butt with his rubber-gloved hand.

Instead of a psalm of praise, I yelled with terror and for the next four decades I stumbled through life thinking it was God who hit me because of something terrible I had done or something terrible that I would do. Happily, I was wrong. At last, after all these years, I have discovered God's smile and heard God's laughter once again.

I'm so glad the memories came back to me. Never again, will I forget the angel, Grace, and Demion, the little devil who drew my name, and all the other angels and devils, cherubim and seraphim, grumps, ghouls, and ghosties, and the archangels and archdemons I met along the way. This is their story really, and the story of millions of God's Lesbian, Gay, Bisexual, Transgender, Queer and Questioning persons just like me whose lives were rescued in the war zone by Grace, the toughest little angel of them all.

Queer Bashing 101 – The Adolescent Years

"We are here to master the art of soul murder, with a special interest in the souls God's Queer Children."

Archdemon Fury

DEMION

Archdemon Fury took his place at a classroom in Hell where the desks steam and the walls sweat. As he placed his asbestos-lined lunchbox under his chair and arranged his notes on the lectern, the Archdemon was humming his favorite hymn:

"You've got to be taught to hate and fear,
You've got to be taught from year to year,
It's got to be drummed in your dear little ear,
You've got to be carefully taught."

Every day, of every year, of every century from the beginning of human time, in that same classroom, that same tenured Archdemon has taught Queer Bashing 101 — The Adolescent Years, a course Satan himself required for all the little devils in his realm. "You're not born to hate," he explained, "You have to learn it and the learning starts in hell."

"Bad morning, class," the Archdemon said happily.

"Bad morning, professor," all the eager demons replied.

"We are here to master the art of soul murder, with a special interest in the souls of God's Queer Children." His grinning students, led by Demion, the teacher's pet, were dry-salivating with anticipation.

"Why you little devil," the Archdemon whispered in Demion's direction, "just a pup and already evil to the core." Demion responded with his most seductive smile.

"Save it," the Archdemon shouted as he slapped his favorite student with the back of his scabby hand. "Use your charm up there to tempt the innocent but don't waste your evil talents on me." Demion turned redder. The class cheered.

Actually, Demion didn't look evil. He was really quite cute, on his way to being handsome. He was a bit taller than the other demons and a natural born leader. The Archdemon knew that if given the chance Demion could charm a pitchfork out of the scaly hands of Satan himself. Already his professor was picturing what this sexy young demon could accomplish with his flashing brown eyes, spiky hair, quick wits, a tightly muscled body, and the natural, inborn instincts of a bully. The Archdemon grinned to himself as he imagined the gay lives Demion could ruin up there where so many young gay men, cut off from family and friends, were dying to be loved.

"Dying to be loved," the Archdemon whispered to himself, "and in the loving, dying." He smiled proudly at his subtle reference to the virus devastating so many of God's gay children. He knew that sex was one of the Creator's gifts to humankind but he also knew how easily the gift became a curse for young homosexuals whose need to understand and express their God-given feelings was met with ignorance and intolerance by family and friends.

Finally the Archdemon regained his professorial pose and turned to face his students who though confused by their teacher's inappropriate cackle and weird mumblings still waited eagerly, pencils in hand.

"Because you are all new at this trade," he said, "Satan in all his wisdom has given you an easy mark, God's homofolk."

Suddenly, he whirled to the blackboard and began to write. Even while the two words hissed and steamed before them, he mouthed each syllable with a sneer.

"A-do-les-cent ho-mo-sex-uals."

While the little demons wrote the two words at the top of their notebooks, their professor moved to the overhead projector and flipped on the light. The students blinked and turned away far more comfortable in the smoky darkness.

"Say it with me," the Archdemon ordered and the class shouted in unison:

"A-do-les-cent ho-mo-sex-uals!"

The little demons still didn't understand the meaning of those two long words or the significance of their calling but the professor didn't pause. "These are other names we use to shame them," the Archdemon said, pointing at the list that glowed before them. "Repeat them after me."

"Faggot," he growled with such menace that the little red hairs on the backs of their little red necks stood up straight.

"Faggot," they replied, doing their best to growl as he growled and curl their lips as he curled his.

"Fairy," he said in his fiendish falsetto, mincing and dancing about the room.

"Fairy," they sang back, giggling, waving limp wrists and tilting their heads as he tilted his.

"Queen, sissy, fruit, homo" he continued sarcastically, rushing down through the names on his list. They echoed each name in reply.

"Dyke," he shouted and the word sounds like a gun shot.

"Diesel dyke," added the professor with a look of disgust.

"Bull dyke," the class read in unison and then broke into laughter and applause.

For a moment, the Archdemon stood silently before them, reveling in their cruelty and contempt for God's Queer Children. Then he turned to the board and wrote his favorite slur.

"So-do-mites," he said gleefully, carefully pronouncing each syllable of that ancient epithet.

"So-do-mites," the little demons repeated with such vigor and contempt that even the Archdemon shivered.

"So-do-mites, so-do-mites," they screamed again and again, dancing around the room, making ugly faces and filthy gestures at that name that hissed and sizzled on the wall. "So-do-mites, so-do-mites!" It became a kind of chant that echoed to the world above.

Where preachers and televangelists were repeating it into television cameras and radio microphones; where boys with paint cans sprayed it on the walls of a synagogue and the windows of a Metropolitan Community Church; where men in white hoods picked up the chant on the lawn where a cross was burning; where a group of skin-heads was beating and kicking to death a young man with a pink triangle pinned to his jacket.

Finally, the Archdemon had to pound on his lectern for order. "There are ugly names for God's Queer ones in English, Spanish, German, French, Japanese, Chinese, Russian and more," he said and without a pause continued adding more ugly names to the list until every country, every tribe, every language was included by the teacher and his mocking, little chorus of devils as they rehearsed their ancient litany of hate.

The Night God Smiled

For the first time in a long, long while, God had smiled and the universe trembled in anticipation of what might happen next.

Archangel Gabriel

GRACE

"**W**here is Abba tonight?" a tough little angel asked the Archangel Gabriel.

"God is walking behind the House on the High Hill," Gabriel replied, whispering God's name and lowering his head in reverence. The Archangel knew how angry and grief-stricken the Creator became when "sodomite," "faggot," or "fairy" echoed up to heaven from the world below.

"I need to see Abba," the zealous, under-sized angel demanded, this time rather brusquely.

If the Archangel hadn't sensed her genuine if inappropriate sincerity, he might have sent her away. After all, he was in a terrible hurry. A conference of the Elders had been called. God was really angry this time and Gabriel was needed on the scene to use his special gifts to help calm the Creator.

But the Archangel knew better than to rush past one of God's little ones. She had called God "Abba" or "daddy." The word itself would have stopped Gabriel in his tracks. Almost 2,000 years earlier, Jesus, himself, had used that informal Aramaic word to name His heavenly Father. It was strictly forbidden, on heaven or on earth, for spiritual leaders to ignore the honest cry for help by any child of God, no matter how small or seemingly unimportant.

So Gabriel sighed, knelt down on the golden street and looked into the determined gaze of this pint-sized, freckled-faced, curly-headed angel who was more at home in faded jeans and a T-shirt than in her regulation garb.

"And I have to see Abba now," she said, crossing her arms tightly and stamping one sandaled foot against the pavement.

Already dozens of curious angels were gathering to see why the highest ranking angel in heaven was kneeling before a rather ordinary angel-in-training on the streets of gold.

"Why do you want to see Abba?" Gabriel asked quietly, anxious to be on his way and bothered by the curious multitude that was gathering.

Seeing the growing crowd of angels, Grace felt very small indeed. Embarrassed and slightly frightened by the sudden, unwanted attention, she disappeared behind Gabriel's dazzling wings.

"Love to you all," said Gabriel addressing the angels who were gathering.

"And love to you," they answered in a single voice that sounded like the music wind makes when it moves gently through the trees in a great forest.

"Will you excuse us, please," Gabriel said flexing his wings just enough to reveal Grace more annoyed by the crowd than frightened. Without a moment's hesitation, the curious angels disappeared.

"What is your name, young one?" he asked.

Peeking around Gabriel's flowing robes and breathing a sigh of relief that they were alone again, the undersized, but tightly muscled little angel replied, "My name is Grace."

"And why do you want to see Abba?" Gabriel asked again.

Grace looked into the kindly eyes of that great, towering figure bathed in light and said softly, "Because when I saw Abba late this afternoon, I thought our Creator was lonely or very, very sad."

For a moment, Gabriel stared at Grace in thoughtful silence. At any other time, the Archangel would have mumbled words of comfort and blessing before sending Grace away. But looking down at this sensitive, determined little angel, Gabriel suddenly realized that Grace might be just what God needed during this lonely, angry time. So, without speaking another word, he took Grace by the hand and together they began their long walk to the Creator's House on the High Hill.

God often came to rest there after a busy day rescuing, reviving and renewing the people on earth. It was the Creator's place to meditate upon creation and the mess the created ones had made of it. Before many minutes passed, Gabriel and Grace saw their Creator, leaning down over the parapets of heaven, looking sadly at the world below. A Council of the Elders stood nearby. As Gabriel approached with Grace in tow, he could see God's grief reflected in the Elder's eyes.

"See," Grace whispered excitedly. "Abba is sad, just as I thought."

"Shhh," the Archangel whispered, hoping the Elders hadn't noticed her lapse in heavenly protocol.

No one in the inner circle ever interrupted God during these moments of terrible sadness. What words would bring comfort to the Creator looking down on all creation, grieving that things had gone so wrong? What action would console the loving maker of humankind as long as evil had such power in the hearts and minds of those God loved?

Even the Archangel Gabriel and the Council of Elders could only stand in helpless silence while their Creator grieved. They were convinced that there was nothing they could say or do to make God smile in the face of such sadness.

"Abba?" little Grace cried out as she scampered past them towards the Creator of the Universe, "why are you crying?"

At the sound of her voice the Elders turned pale. The Archangel rushed to pull the tough, little angel away. At that same moment, God heard Grace and turned to see the little one kneeling there. There was something about Grace that won God's heart immediately.

"At this moment," Abba said, looking into the eyes of Grace and marveling at her courage. "I am crying for my Queer Children."

"Why are you crying for them?" asked the innocent angel.

"Because they are suffering," Abba answered softly, "and they think I do not care."

"Why ever would they think that?" Grace asked indignantly, her dark flashing eyes filled with surprise.

The Creator was silent. Even the question broke God's heart. Then, after a long pause, Abba took Grace by the hand and led her to the very edge of heaven.

"Listen," the Creator whispered and in that heavenly stillness. Grace could hear angry voices echoing up from the earth, dozens, maybe hundreds, even thousands of them, condemning voices, unloving voices, voices filled with sneering contempt for God's Queer Children.

"Night and day, I hear their voices," Abba said sadly, "denouncing my Queerfolk falsely, misusing the Writings to berate them, inflaming their friends and families against them, imprisoning them under false charges or torturing them with false 'cures.' How could my Homofolk know that I love them when the air is filled with these condemning voices?"

"Why don't you tell them yourself?" Grace asked.

"I have," God replied quietly, looking down across that long distance to the earth and remembering the prophets, the martyrs, the manger, cross, and empty tomb.

"Tell them again," Grace almost shouted and the Archangel, thinking her impudence had gone far enough, rushed to take charge of that noisy little angel. Instead, the Creator motioned him away.

"I think I will!" God said suddenly, reaching for a giant lightning bolt and throwing it like a javelin towards the earth. Seconds later, God's hands smacked together with such force that it sounded like a booming clap of thunder.

Down below, television screens carrying the sermons of preachers and priests condemning "sodomites" to hell, flickered and went dark. The radio broadcasts of anti-Gay politicians on witch-hunts were interrupted by noisy static before they, too, went off the air. Simultaneously, sound systems went out with the lights in large churches, lecture halls, and political rallies where sexual and gender minorities were being vilified. For one blessed moment all those false and inflammatory voices were silenced across the land.

And in that sudden silence, God leaned out over space and said with a voice that all creation could hear, "I love my Queer Children!"

"Do you think they'll hear it?" the Grace asked quietly.

"They will," God answered, "if they are listening."

At that moment, Grace saw in the eyes of God a look so full of love that it made a shiver run up and down her spine.

"I love you, too," she said softly, standing on her tip toes to kiss her Creator gently on the cheek.

The spontaneous rush of love that flowed out of Grace broke through God's anger and grief. At that very moment, the Creator of the Universe had a brilliant idea. If Grace could make such a difference in the life of her Creator what might she do in the lives of God's Queerfolk? Just thinking about adding Grace to the elite corps of angels assigned to guide and guard them gave the Creator another surge of joy.

Seeing the amazing change in God's eyes, the Archangel and the Elders dropped to their knees and a million angels burst into song. The heavens above them filled with dancing lights and the people living in the broken, bleeding world below, billions of them, strained heavenward to see and hear the wonder in the sky. For the first time in a long, long while, God had smiled and the universe trembled in anticipation of what might happen next.

"They Are Different!"

Satan walked among them, whispering, "They are different." And it wasn't long until that evil whisper once again had won the day.

Archdemon Fury

DEMION

At that very moment, the Archdemon was beginning his favorite lesson in Queer Bashing 101 – The Adolescent Years.

"Ho-mo-pho-bia," he chortled, burning the word, letter by sizzling letter, with one bony, blazing finger on to the classroom wall.

"Homo," he sneered, underlining the first four letters with a slash of contempt, "God's Queer ones."

The class booed and hissed on cue.

"Phobia," the Archdemon shouted over the bedlam, "another word for fear."

"Fear!" the class yelled back in unison.

Suddenly the Archdemon lowered his voice to a whisper. "Homophobia," he said, "Queer-fear."

All the little devils but Demion dutifully scribbled the definition into their thickening red notebooks. He was chewing the end of his asbestos pencil and looking rather confused.

"Why should anyone be afraid of God's Queer ones?" he blurted out, surprised that God's homofolk could strike fear into anyone's heart.

The Archdemon shrieked with laughter.

"You got it, boy," the old geezer shouted happily, moving up the aisle to pound Demion on the shoulder. "Ho-mo-pho-bia: To fear God's homofolk with absolutely no real reason to fear them."

The Archdemon sat down on Demion's desk and the class leaned forward to listen. They loved to hear their professor's ancient stories of Satan at work long before recorded time.

"Satan launched his Fear the Queer Campaign ages before these stories were even written down, in the village of Nippur where the Tigris and Euphrates Rivers flow together into the Persian Gulf. Picture it! Friends and family were gathering to celebrate the love of two young warriors."

"Ugh," Demion muttered under his fetid breath not even knowing why he felt disgusted.

"In those ancient, pre-historic days," the Archdemon hissed, "no one thought it strange for two men or two women to love each other. Weddings were held. Families exchanged gifts. The lovers, of the same or opposite sex, were carried to their marriage bed on the shoulders of their friends."

The little demons whispered among themselves excitedly and shook their heads in disbelief.

"On that same day, the Prince of Darkness happened by Nippur."

The demons cheered and jumped up and down with anticipation.

"Lucifer smelled fresh wheat cakes," the Archdemon added, "and the unmistakable fragrance of freshly picked flowers and newly fermented grapes. He heard the sound of flutes and drums, then voices raised in song. It was a party and you know how much our Lord and Master hates parties. They signal happiness and Satan's one true goal is to destroy happiness whenever he discovers it."

The demons booed, hissed and stamped their feet at the very mention of happiness. Satan had made it clear — a happy queer is a dangerous queer. It's so much easier to steal an unhappy soul.

"Back to the story," the Archdemon interrupted raising his hand for silence. "On that wedding day, Satan stood at the back of the happy crowd of villagers, watching the two young men draped in garlands of leaves and flowers, holding hands, and exchanging poetic promises. Then, it came to him. They are different from the norm and just being different makes them vulnerable to rumors, half-truths, and lies."

That seemed important enough that even Demion began to take notes.

"Inspired by the possibilities, Satan leaned forward and whispered into the ear of an old villager standing nearby. 'They are different,' he had sneered in his most ominous tones and before long the whisper spread among the villagers. 'They are different.' 'They are different.' 'They are different.' Slowly the mood changed from celebration to suspicion, from suspicion to fear, from fear to hatred, and from hatred to violent rage."

The demons leaned forward. Demion felt the palms of his hands and the tips of his pointed little ears grow hot with anticipation.

"In the terrible grip of Satan's lying whisper, the hysterical crowd of villagers attacked the two young warriors, kicking and beating them mercilessly. For a moment, the lovers fought for their lives, wondering why their love for each other had caused their friends and families to turn against them. Bleeding and knowing they were about to die, the two young men embraced one last time. Infuriated by their embrace, that crowd of friends and family stoned the boys to death."

The Archdemon paused to take a breath while the little devils cheered.

"Instead of marrying the two young lovers that day," the Archdemon continued, "their friends and families prepared to bury them. While the women anointed the bodies of the boys they had known since childhood, they began to ask themselves 'why?' While the men built the large wooden coffin and dug the common grave, they, too, wondered 'why?'"

"'Why did we suddenly think of them as different, just because they loved each other?' 'Why did we fear the difference?' 'Why did we attack and kill them when all they wanted was to share their love with us?'"

"By the time the muffled drum played and the chant of grief was sung the villagers were weeping in the market place. Satan knew that something had to be done quickly before the people came to their senses. So, once again, he walked among the mourners whispering, 'But they were different.' And it wasn't long until that evil whisper once again had won the day."

"Ho-mo-pho-bia," the Archdemon hissed happily. "To fear God's Queer Children just because they are different."

"Ho-mo-pho-bia," Demion repeated to himself, writing each word into his tattered notebook.

"Ho-mo-pho-bia," the Archdemon hissed again. "BECAUSE," he said, "Satan knows that fearing God's Queer Children always leads to hating them."

"Ho-mo-pho-bia," the little demons said in almost perfect unison. "BECAUSE Satan knows that fearing God's Queer Children always leads to hating them."

"Well done," the Archdemon ordered. "Now put down your pencils and listen! To spread the rumor effectively you can't just say 'They are different.' You have to whisper it like this. 'They...are...different,'" Fury whispered.

"They...are...different," the demons whispered back.

"No! No! No!" the Archdemon shouted, "To succeed in spreading our Master's rumor, you must learn the Master's whisper."

The little demons looked at each other in confusion.

"Stand up!" old Fury shouted impatiently and Demion and his classmates scrambled from their desks, spilling notebooks and dropping pencils in the process.

"Attention!" the Archdemon screamed and his frightened students snapped into formation, chins up, bellies in, chests thrust forward, arms stiff at their sides.

"Repeat after me," the Devil's favorite henchman commanded and the rank of little devils shouted back in unison, "Yes, SIR!"

For a moment there was silence. Archdemon Fury walked slowly back and forth before them. His eyes were closed. His lips were moving silently, like an actor back stage rehearsing his lines before rushing on stage to deliver them. Suddenly, when he thought he had it just right, the wizened old demon grinned and whirled to face them.

"They ... are ... different," he whispered and the little devils were stunned by the sound of it. The voice wasn't at all like the Archdemon's voice. Demion struggled to remember where he had heard that sound before. Then, suddenly, he knew. It was exactly like the voice of God, or a very close copy, riding on the Archdemon's stinking breath. It had a touch of God's gentle, loving voice, tinged with the Devil's own menace. It was a dangerous, deadly lie masquerading as God's own truth. And the power of the lie was compounded by the god-like delivery of the Father of all Lies.

"On the surface," Archdemon Fury explained, "'they are different' must sound sympathetic, concerned, almost compassionate, but just below the surface," he added with a grin, "you must make your listeners believe that 'the different ones' are evil, a menace, a threat to society that must not be tolerated."

Once again, the old Archdemon spoke the words that sounded like love but led directly to intolerance.

"They ... are ... different," Fury whispered again and for a moment he reveled in his perfect delivery as those three terrible words echoed about the room. The Archdemon had mastered his Master's voice. It had taken centuries. Satan himself had coached Fury in this difficult and demanding delivery.

"The lie must sound like Truth," the Prince of Lies had told him, "God's truth. It must sound like love," he added, "but it must lead to hate."

"Now, you try it," the Archdemon commanded the little devils in his class and Demion and his friends answered with immediate, military precision, "They are different, SIR!"

"No!" old Fury screamed. "Listen!"

A fourth time there was silence as the Archdemon closed his eyes and took three deep, hacking breaths to center his surly, sullen soul. Then, pursing his lips and smiling broadly, he whispered gently but with a terrible underlying menace, "They ... are ... different."

The demons were so moved by their professor's delivery that they broke into spontaneous applause. For the rest of that day and long into the night, one by one they stood before him, mouthing those terrible words that lead to the suffering and death of God's Queer Children until each and every demon had mastered the Master's voice.

"They ... are ... different." "They ... are ... different." "They ... are ... different."

(VI)

"Send Grace!"

"The entire heavenly host watched in silence as God lifted that tiny human form that would grow to be one of the Creator's own Trans children and for a long and loving moment held her close."

St. Peter

GRACE

High above that hellish scene, the Archangel Gabriel rushed through the golden streets of heaven, holding tightly to the hand of Grace. She was athletic and in robust good health, but her legs were short and he was practically running. For every giant step Gabriel took, Grace took three quick hops. In fact, that tough but undersized angel bobbed and twirled behind the Archangel like a child's balloon tied to the bumper of a speeding bus. There were times she barely touched the ground, and the seraphim and cherubim who saw them rush past struggled to keep from laughing at the sight.

"Where are we going?" Grace gasped, confused by the sudden turn of events. At one moment she had been holding Abba's hand looking down on the earth from the very edge of heaven. Seconds later, Gabriel was almost dragging her through the crowded golden streets.

Gabriel knew that Grace was not ready to hear, let alone to understand the tragic history of God's Queerfolk: Stoned to death in antiquity, burned alive during the medieval era, and hanged from gallows until the mid-1800s, even in modern times, sexual and gender minorities continue to be the victims of groundless religious dogma. To feel condemned and rejected by their pastors, priests and rabbis makes them feel condemned and rejected by their Creator and that leads to wasted lives, ruined relationships, divided families, physical, emotional, and spiritual violence and even death.

Gabriel was baffled by the Creator's decision to send Grace. For centuries, the special angels assigned to guide and guard God's Queerfolk had been frustrated by failure. Grace was tough, but what could she do to help combat centuries of bigotry, violence, and death when a legion of other angels had failed?

The Archangel was also surprised by God's response to his doubts about Grace. "Don't worry," God had said looking with confidence at the newly appointed angel. "My Grace is sufficient." Gabriel was shocked. Had God just made a pun, the lowest form of humor?

"Hold it!" Grace said skidding to a sudden stop as Gabriel led her quite unexpectedly down an all-too-familiar pathway. Arms folded, eyes squinting daggers, she turned her back on the campus stretching out before them. "I'm not going back to school," she growled and Gabriel could see in the flashing, determined eyes of Grace that the decision was final.

Infant angels, newly created and unequipped for duty, are trained in a kind of angel boot camp in the shadows of the Pearly Gates. Grace had unhappy memories of those classroom days. She wasn't eager to repeat them.

"You've been chosen for a very important mission," the Archangel said with quiet determination, "and you'll need special training to accomplish it."

Grace dug in and refused to budge. Once again Gabriel wondered why God had chosen this stubborn, strong-willed angel to join the distinguished band of specialists on assignment as guardians of God's Homofolk. During their brief, whispered conversation near God's House on the high hill, Gabriel had urged the Creator to reconsider, but God just smiled, patted him gently on the arm, and repeated his command: "Send Grace."

Seeing the determined look in Grace's flashing eyes, Gabriel sighed with resignation, sat down on a marble bench in the shadow of Old Main, and invited Grace to sit beside him.

"I already graduated from this dump," Grace said, plopping down beside him, rifling frantically through the messy knapsack she always carried. "See," she shouted triumphantly, holding up a smudged and wrinkled paper with the school's official seal clearly embossed in blue and gold.

Thousands of those diplomas, beautifully framed and mounted, hung on the walls of angel apartments and offices all over heaven. Grace hadn't bothered. She didn't want to be reminded of her class- room days. Besides, the diploma wouldn't look right on her office wall, mounted among her prized collection of screw drivers, hand saws, ratchet wrenches, and other special tools she had requisitioned for her work.

Grace loved her handy person's job in heaven's maintenance de- partment and hoped never to be promoted. Other angels thrived on continuing education courses or even grad school while Grace enjoyed the feel of a smooth, wooden hammer in her hands as she balanced precariously on the roof of a heavenly mansion, replacing tiles that had been blown away in a sudden summer storm.

"Grace," a familiar voice interrupted the awkward silence. The toughest little angel in heaven was suddenly transformed. She jumped to her feet, bowed low and, still kneeling, looked up into the face of St. Peter, the headmaster of that Heavenly finishing school. She smiled bashfully.

"Hi, Pete," Grace whispered, looking down at her dirty fingernails and turning quite red in the process. Gabriel couldn't help notice that in spite of the irreverence implicit in her greeting, her hoarse, boyish voice had a friendly, almost reverential tone.

The campus had been erected near the Pearly Gates for the con- venience of St. Peter himself. When he wasn't greeting heaven's new arrivals, he liked to walk up and down the infant angels' diminutive ranks, fingering the whistle at his neck, writing notes on his clipboard and shouting firm but gentle commands to his tiny troops.

However, unlike drill sergeants at Camp Pendleton or Perris Is- land, St. Peter has been seen kneeling near the hurdles, wiping tears from the face of a fallen angel or even arriving back in camp after an exhausting five mile run with the entire angelic troop riding on his shoulders or clinging tightly to his robe and nodding sleepily.

"Thank you," St. Peter said to Gabriel. "I'll take Grace the rest of the way."

As the Archangel Gabriel stood to move away, he was amazed to see stubborn Grace reach up to grip St. Peter's extended hand and, without another word of protest, walk with him through the gates and down the campus pathway.

Grace had hated her school years, each and every miserable day of them; but she loved "Pete" and trusted him. When the other angelic faculty had insisted she be expelled, the headmaster had refused to comply. He encouraged Grace, tutoring her on the side, letting her plow and plant with the gardeners when the other angels were playing harps or singing the sacred oratorios. And when she didn't grow tall and graceful like the rest, St. Peter let Grace spend extra time in the gym, lifting weights and building muscle to compensate.

Now, the headmaster himself was walking Grace across the campus like an honored alumnus returning to deliver a homecoming address or receive an honorary degree. And all the cherub students who passed by wondered who she was and why St. Peter, headmaster and co-founder of this special place, was showing her such deference.

Neither Grace nor Saint Peter said a word. They walked together silently, hand-in-hand, past the built-to-scale barracks and classrooms where the infant angels lived and studied, the library filled with tiny, ancient scrolls, the miniature soccer field, the peewee exercise course, and the archery range where ranks of tiny cupids in over-sized diapers and freshly shined halos were shooting arrows at targets shaped like human hearts.

"Here we are," St. Peter said cheerfully as they walked along a pathway towards the ivy-covered, wrought-iron gates of Eden, chained shut shortly after the beginning of time.

"We can't go in there," Grace whispered. "It's off limits."

Before St. Peter could respond, a seraph stepped from a stone guardhouse nearly hidden in a tangle of ivy. The imposing angelic presence raised her wings to block their way.

"See," Grace said, pulling on St. Peter's arm. "I told you."

The seraph towered over them. One of the highest orders of celestial beings, the seraphim act as God's Secret Service, a kind of honor guard, hovering above the throne, commissioned to stand watch over the places, real and holy-graphic, that God loves best, the private places where the Creator is apt to spend time alone, contemplating creation.

"Open the gate, please," St. Peter said softly, but the seraph didn't move, she just looked down at Grace and scowled slightly.

It was the Jewish prophet, Isaiah, who first described the seraphim in his stunning vision of God's heavenly throne, "high and lifted-up." Unlike two-winged Grace, who often tangled her short feathered appendages in the simplest flying exercise, the seraphim had six wings, two above, two below, and one on each side; and they could fan the air furiously with one pair, furl and unfurl another, and hover or fly at nearly the speed of sound with the third, all at the very same time. On several occasions during her ill-fated undergraduate days, Grace had cut class and wandered down to these "off-limit" ivy-covered-gates just to watch the seraphim's precision wing drills during their colorful changing of the guard.

"Hey there, Six Wings," Grace said glowering up at the sentry. "Didn't you hear the man?"

The seraph was not amused.

"We've been invited by our Creator to visit this holy place," St. Peter said quietly. Recognizing the voice of one of heaven's highest officials, the seraph bowed low, and slowly rose above them, moving in silent majesty to unlock and open the gates. Grace grinned up at St. Peter and gripped his hand tightly as the chains fell away. She had always wanted to wander down the pathways of this mysterious garden paradise.

On those lovely truant days away from class and library when the seraph sentries had their backs turned, Grace had sneaked up through the nearly impenetrable wall of high, flowering grass, thick bush and overhanging trees, pulled apart the tangle of wild ivy and peered through the iron fence that encircled Eden.

None of the other cherubs believed Grace when she told them what she had seen in that forbidden place: the trees laden with bright red, orange, and yellow fruit; the colorful birds that sang, cawed and cackled; and the family of deer that drank from the clear-as-crystal stream just before it disappeared into the dark, green forest. And though she had never dared to disobey the "Keep Out" sign, Grace was curious to know why such a beautiful place would be "Closed by God's command."

Saint Peter led Grace across the stream, through a corner of the forest and into a clearing where a second seraph stood guard. The clearing was flickering with light from a bright fire that burned with the intensity of a sunburst, rays radiating out from its core like sunbeams piercing the darkness. Grace fell to her knees, almost overwhelmed by the heat and light of that flame. Saint Peter knelt beside her. The woods were silent. Nothing moved. Another of the seraphim stood at attention nearby.

"What happened here?" Grace whispered.

"Just wait, Grace," Peter responded gently. "In God's good time you shall know."

It didn't take long for Grace to grow restless. After staring at the flame for two or three full minutes, she began to look around the clearing. There was nothing special about it, just a flat, brown, circle of dirt on the edge of a tiny stream in the shadows of a great, unkempt garden. Except for the hot, bright flame, there was nothing about that clearing that made it special.

"In God's good time," the old Saint said again, sensing her growing restlessness. "In God's good..."

Without warning the seraph sentry's three sets of powerful wings began to fan the air. They made a kind of music, like the high pitched sound of an approaching summer storm. The sentry's alarm was answered by other seraphim fanning their wings on guard at the front gate and down the winding paths of Eden. Within seconds, the entire garden echoed with the sounds of celebration. Grace jumped to her feet just as God appeared at the edge of the clearing with an entourage of angels and archangels moving swiftly in her direction.

"Hello, Grace," God said, taking the angel's eager hand, leading her across the clearing, and sitting beside her on a fallen log near that bright, blazing light. For the first time, Grace had nothing to say. She was terrified and at the same time confident that all would be explained as St. Peter had assured her "in God's good time."

"These are new arrivals," God explained, motioning a small group of spirits to join them near the fire. "They are scientists with questions," God added smiling, "questions almost as profound as your own."

"What happened here?" Grace stammered. "Why is this place so special?"

God didn't answer right away. Instead, the Creator of all things great and small leaned down and scooped up a handful of damp sand from the bank of that swiftly flowing stream.

Grace blinked hard and focused on the small mound of mud being shaped by God's swiftly moving fingers. Then just as God bent down to breathe on that little wad of clay, an amazing thing happened. Those grains of sand that had seemed hard and lifeless on the beach pulsed with life in the Creator's warm and loving hands.

"You mean it's true?" one of the new arrivals asked trying hard to conceal her skepticism.

"Human life actually began here?" another added.

"With a handful of clay," a third scientist gasped, "that you shaped with your fingers?"

"Why not?" God replied, winking at Grace. "I love the story, don't you?"

For a moment, there was silence. And in that very silence, demonic voices were heard echoing through the garden from the steaming core of hell. Demion and the other little demons in Queer Bashing 101 were dancing around the Archdemon repeating their homophobic chorus, "They are different! They are different! They are different!"

Grace trembled at the angry look that suddenly appeared in her Creator's eyes. She had seen that look before when the cries of "faggot," "fairy," and "sodomite" echoed from the earth interrupting the peace of heaven and breaking the heart of God.

"That's why I wanted you here," God said to Grace, showing that tough little angel the handful of glowing sand, whirling with protons, neutrons, and electrons, each blazing with the breath of life. "Every newborn child from the beginning of time to this very day was shaped by my own hands! And that includes all my Queer Children each and every one."

"But they are different," one of the new arrivals dared to suggest.

"Of course, they're different," God exclaimed. "But that difference is something to celebrate, not condemn."

God's voice rumbled across the heavens. The Creator was angry and the crowd of angels and archangels bowed low and waited for the anger to pass. One of the new arrivals, oblivious to heavenly decorum, interrupted the silence with a question that scientists in heaven and on earth were asking.

"How exactly do you make each one of them different from the other?" she asked. "It would make us all so happy to know."

God and Grace sat side-by-side in silence, staring with fascination at the wad of clay, ablaze with life, in the palm of the Creator's hand. The curious and impatient scientists clustered around the log, trying to postpone politely the questions they longed to ask. Finally, the bravest of the bunch asked boldly, "Is sexual orientation genetic? Will they isolate the Gay marker in the Xq28 region of the X chromosome and find the secret?"

God just smiled and continued looking down at Grace who couldn't take her eyes off the sparkling, moving mass in her Creator's hand.

"Or is it the size of the hypothalamus or the anterior commissure that makes the difference?" a second new arrival asked.

Again, God did not reply and the Creator's silence made the scientists all the more anxious for answers.

"Or is it predetermined by prenatal hormonal levels?" another questioned, "or by some mysterious combination of events that happen during infancy?"

Suddenly, God replied. "It is nature, one of you has said, and it is nurture," God added, "Can't you be satisfied with your own answer? It makes perfect sense to me."

"But will we ever unlock the secret combination?" someone asked.

"I hope not," the Creator said, remembering painfully the attempts that have been made over the last century to discover the "missing gene" not to celebrate God's Queerfolk but to destroy them even before they were born.

The new arrivals nodded their heads in sad agreement, knowing how hard they had worked to discover the secrets of sexual orientation and gender identity; and yet, how worried they too had been that once discovered the secret would be used to alter or even abolish the difference.

"Don't worry," God said. "There is one last step in the creation of my Queer Children that no one can alter or abolish."

Without saying another word, the Creator stood up and walked to the center of the clearing.

"It is almost time," God said, still looking with love at the tiny form taking shape miraculously before their eyes. "This very special child of mine is almost ready for her journey!"

God nodded to Gabriel. Instantly, the Archangel summoned an angel messenger to stand at God's right hand.

"Now," God said, looking at Grace, but speaking loud enough for all the new arrivals to hear. "Now you will see what truly makes them different, the secret that no one will ever discover or destroy."

At that moment every angel and archangel in God's heavenly entourage knelt before their Creator. The only sound heard in the garden was the music of a thousand seraph wings, beating in a kind of drum roll signaling the main event. The scientists watched as their question was about to be answered at last. Grace trembled with excitement.

Slowly God lifted that tiny human form that would grow to be one of the Creator's very special Transgender Children and for a long and loving moment held her close. While God held her there, the eternal fire suddenly blazed in the clearing. The heavenly host joined their voices in a hymn of praise. And Grace, still looking into the eyes of God, saw such compassion there that her heart nearly exploded.

Then, with one final embrace, God handed the new creation to an angelic messenger who took the child in her hands, bowed low, and disappeared in a flash of light towards the earth below.

Instantly God and the heavenly host disappeared leaving Grace and Saint Peter alone in the clearing still lit by the blazing fire. God's sudden appearance and then God's equally sudden disappearance left Grace dizzy.

"Was it a dream?" she asked St. Peter. "Was God really here? Did I see the Creator actually make a Transgender child? What is Transgender anyway?"

"You'll understand what Transgender means …"

"I know," Grace interrupted, "in God's good time. But they must be very special."

"Why do you say that?" Peter asked.

Grace didn't answer. When she spoke her normally gruff little voice was charged with emotion. "It was something about the way the Creator held that little lump of life," she said, "and how God held it for so long."

Peter smiled, took Grace by the hand and led her back towards the gated entrance to the garden.

"All God's Children are special," St. Peter explained. "But God holds Transgender Children a little longer because they will need extra strength and courage down there where their friends and family may not understand."

"Pete," Grace asked, "does God hold every new child that way?"

St. Peter paused. "In many tribes," he continued, "in many lands, Transgender people have been called 'the two spirited ones.'"

Grace looked confused. Peter tried to explain."Over the centuries," he said, "these 'two spirited ones' have often been chosen as spiritual leaders because they were seen to bridge the gap between male and female, to have been born with both spirits."

Grace was silent. She was trying to understand. Still not quite sure what it all meant she asked quietly, "Pete, does God hold every new child in a special way?"

Yes," St. Peter replied, "God holds each unborn child in a special way." Then he stopped, knelt down in front of Grace, looked directly into her eyes and added, "Except God holds all the Queer Children just a little longer because God knows they'll need it."

Liar of the Year Awards

*"If God's precious little sodomites ever hear those words," he
mumbled, "if they ever really hear that their Creator loves
them…as they are…all is lost."*

Satan

DEMION

Suddenly, Satan himself rushed into Queer Bashing 101. He was
mad as hell. The Archdemon had never seen the Prince of Darkness quite so unnerved. The entire class ducked down hoping
not to be scorched by his fury.

"God holds the Queer Children just a little longer!" Satan sneered.
The demons hissed at hearing the Creator's name. "God holds the
Queer Children just a little longer," he scoffed again his voice drip-
ping with sarcasm. For a moment Satan paced back and forth furiously. Then he shouted the words a third time, words he hated with all
his heartlessness. "God holds the Queer Children just a little longer."

As those words echoed around the classroom Satan raised his
face to the ceiling and howled like a wolf, scaring the little demons
right under their desks. When the Archdemon approached with a
word of comfort, the Prince of Evil knocked him down with the back
of his horny hand.

"If God's precious little sodomites ever hear those words," he
mumbled, "if they ever really hear that their Creator holds them just
a little longer, that He loves them … exactly as they are … all is lost."

"But we won't let them hear those words," the Archdemon said,
standing to his feet and addressing the class. "Will we students?"

"No," they shouted, over and over again, until Satan himself was convinced. He wiped his eyes and stood before them grinning.

"You will not fail me, will you?" he asked. And again they shouted, "No!"

"Good," Satan answered walking up and down the aisles, patting this one on the head and that one on the shoulder.

"God may love sodomites," Satan muttered happily, "but it will take more than lightning bolts and thunder claps to undo the lies we've invented to use against them."

"So-do-mites!" the demons echoed in a concert of contempt.

"Shut up, you sniveling little freaks," Satan screamed in their direction, hurling more of his fiery little missiles and belching black, acrid smoke that filled the room and left them gasping.

Archdemon lifted his hand for silence. The demon students slunk back into their chairs. The room grew ominously quiet. Finally, Satan spoke again.

"Name calling is not enough to destroy the souls of God's little sodomites," he said slowly. "They are born feeling loved by their Creator," and just before the demons could hiss that name, he added "but as quickly as they are born you must make them forget that God created them and loves them exactly as they are. Your ultimate goal," added Satan, the Father of all Lies in a voice that made the demon's tremble, "is to make them believe that God doesn't love them, never did, never will!"

"Never did! Never will!" the demons echoed. Demion scribbled notes as the Prince of Darkness continued.

"Those nasty little words," Satan explained, "are a quick and dirty way of passing on my beautiful lie." He sneered to himself. "Calling the Queer ones 'fruit' or 'faggot' or 'fairy' is a shortcut for saying 'God doesn't love you as you are' BUT," Satan continued, "you must never use those nasty little words yourselves. Hissing 'fruit' or 'faggot' or 'fairy' may bring joy to your tongue, but you must never say those words, at least not out loud, not up there. No. No. No."

The demons looked confused.

"If God's 'beloved homos' discover that I, Satan, the Prince of Deceit, am the source of those pernicious little nicknames, they will lose their power."

Demion scribbled furiously.

"Hear this, my stupid little fiends," Satan shouted. "You must never torment a Queer yourself," he said, whirling to the blackboard. "Let their families and friends, their teachers, pastors and priests do it for you." He wrote the golden rule of Queer-bashing on the blackboard and then turned to explain.

"Family and friends, pastors and priests might never use the truly nasty nicknames to demean the homos, but they will use other words that work as well. 'Sick!' 'Sinful!' 'Unnatural!' 'Abomination!' It doesn't matter. They're all just different ways of repeating my lie. In fact," Satan added basking in his own brilliance, "it's even worse than calling their homo children 'dykes' or 'faggots' when parents say such things as: 'You're such a disappointment...' or 'We need to find someone who can help you...' or 'You'll grow out of this...' or 'Please don't tell your father...' Those 'harmless' little announcements are in fact a perfect way to disguise the lie that..."

"God doesn't love them as they are," the demons said in perfect sync even before Satan could repeat his favorite lie. Satan smiled knowing that his lie would be carried safely to the world above by this enthusiastic class of young demons.

"Let everyone torture God's Queer Children in their own unique ways, with their own unique words," Satan added. "With just a little encouragement from my allies on earth, radio and TV preachers, politicians, pastors, priests and rabbis will line up to do my work. Even popes, cardinals, bishops and priests will help you. AND I CAN PROVE IT!"

Suddenly his Ugliness turned from them and rushed towards the door. "Follow me!" he shouted over his shoulder and the Archdemon and his class of little demons jumped up from their desks, grabbed their pencils and notebooks and rushed after Satan the Demon-in-Chief.

Before they could catch him, the Devil had entered his own private elevator that could speed him fast as the wind to the basement of hell or to the multipurpose room on the penthouse level of hell's tallest building. In fact, that banquet hall, conference center, and/or ballroom was located so close to the earth's crust that a noisy celebration could shift the earth's plates creating earthquakes, tsunamis and other natural disasters around the world. Hoping to set off another global calamity the demons jumped up and down, jostling and jeering as the freight elevator lifted the entire class in stops and starts to the very top floor of hell.

The Archdemon knew what he might risk leading his unruly class into the invitation-only luncheon about to take place behind the golden doors. "Stop!" he yelled and the demons skidded to a halt on the polished granite floors. The celebration had just begun. Lucifer's favorite fallen angel stepped to the microphone to welcome hell's leading citizens to the Liar of the Year Award Luncheon. Even the Archdemon had not received a coveted invitation to this annual festival of falsehood honoring Satan's favorite lies and favored liars.

The Archdemon rushed into the Red Room hoping to find Satan waiting to make his entrance. Only the Old Man could convince the door devils that this unruly class of demons should be allowed to attend this hallowed happening. To his relief, Satan was there trying to squeeze into his favorite red satin tuxedo but his mood had shifted. Instead of his happy "Follow me!" Satan was staring at himself in the floor-to-ceiling mirrors yelling at the demon tailor who was cringing before him.

"Pleash, shire," the tailor stammered through teeth still clenching a full row of pins, "if you'd shstand shstill shings would go mush fashter."

After another long look into the wall of mirrors, even Satan could see that his tuxedo needed refitting before he could wear it again. His jacket had to be let out to accommodate his corpulent, ever swelling paunch. His pants needed reinforcing to support his ever sagging derrière. And his tail hole needed lowering at least another quarter of an inch.

Giving up, Satan stormed into the banquet hall without changing from his scorched and sooty work clothes. Actually, he was cheered by the thought that wearing them might even help improve his reputation as "hell's most humble" far more than the red satin tux.

The huge room was jam-packed with delirious celebrants who jumped to their feet screaming and applauding as Satan, their Liar-in-Chief, climbed to the dais followed by a dozen high-ranking archdemons and their entourage of toadies and hangers-on. Even Halloween couldn't hold a candle to the excitement of this event. Satan loves lies, the bigger the better, and every year the cream of hell's society dresses up to honor the best lies of the year.

As he basked in the praise of his minions Satan's mood changed again. Now he was smiling broadly, waiting (not impatiently) for the ovation to end. Thankfully Satan noticed the Archdemon and his class of demons standing in the hallway and waved them in. When the room grew quiet Satan lifted his champagne glass and repeated the annual toast, "To lies!" he shouted, "and to the liars who tell them."

As the Prince of Darkness sank back into his throne, he gestured to Samael, his favorite fallen angel to begin the celebration. With a flick of wrist, Samael signaled the stage demons to raise the great, red curtain while house demons lowered the lights. The denizens of hell roared their approval as the wall of mirrors before them burst into life.

"This year," Samael shouted excitedly into the mike, "your five nominees for Liar of the Year include..." For a moment, he paused to look back over his shoulder to see if the media demons would project the right picture on cue. At that very instant the life-sized image of a popular Christian psychologist with a radio show dedicated to the American family appeared on the screen.

"Homosexuals are a threat to this nation's families," he whined into the microphone. "They endanger our homes and prey on our children."

It was a whopper of a lie. Even first year devils knew that God's Queer ones value family life, that they have long-term, loving relationships and children of their own, and that most cases of child molestation occur in heterosexual homes, committed by parents and relatives on their own children. Believing the lie that God's Homofolk are a threat to family, the poor, misinformed Christian psychologist had lied boldly and the great hall of demons erupted into enthusiastic applause at his devilish daring.

Seconds later, live pictures of a Christian television host, bogus news commentator and former U.S. presidential candidate appeared on the screen.

"Homosexual activists have a godless, humanistic scheme to destroy America's traditional moral values," he said with mock authority, "and are determined to destroy all remnants of our Christian faith." Even Satan, who knew there was no such scheme, had to join in their laughter and applause. On Satan's own "to do-in" list were millions of Queer Christians who had kept the faith and served the church in spite of the lies being told against them. Satan smiled at the irony. Unwittingly this sincere and well-meaning televangelist had helped divide Christendom and do the Devil's business. The demons clapped and stomped their approval.

Immediately, the third nominee appeared life-sized on their screen. Wearing combat ribbons and an infectious grin, a famous American general leaned into a microphone before a Senate Committee and spoke against the decision to allow Gays and Lesbians into the military.

"It was a terrible mistake to allow homosexuals into the armed forces," he declared. "Their lifestyle is incompatible with military service."

Satan and his friends cheered this tired old lie, glad for all the suffering it had brought to courageous homos in service of their country, grateful that the general still believed that there is such a thing as a "Gay life style" when in fact, the lives of God's Queer Children are as responsible and as diverse as the general population. Right there in the Senate hearing room broadcast to the world on CNN, the "reluctant warrior" had betrayed his troops with that devastating lie and the devils screamed with delight.

Seconds later, the fourth nominee, a popular southern television preacher, appeared life-like on the screen.

"AIDS is God's punishment for homosexuals," the television preacher shouted into the microphone, and the crowd went wild. This, certainly, was the lie of the year, of the decade, of the century. Even Satan was standing and cheering after that preacher blasphemed his own loving Creator on network television. Even the demons knew that HIV was a virus and that God loves everyone with the virus as much as God loves those without it. "We can't compete with that," Satan yelled above the chaos, while the chief fallen angel thumped and shouted for order.

Finally, the enthusiastic crowd settled down to watch the image of the last nominee that year. A matronly woman who headed one of America's largest Christian women's political organizations appeared on the screen. The crowd of demons sighed. They knew in their ugly, little hearts that she was just a token nominee. Satan was the original sexist, and though he insisted on being politically correct on these public occasions, he was absolutely certain that no woman could lie as well as a man. How could she compete with that crowd of brilliant male liars and their brilliant male lies?

"God hates Gays," the gray-haired woman said with a sly, half smile as she held up a little leather book and spoke again. "The Bible tells me so."

For a moment a stunned silence hung over the jam-packed banquet hall. The demons were blown away by the beauty, the simplicity, the perfection of that lie. Even Satan sat in his throne gasping with surprise. It was one thing to lie about God, but it was pure genius to wave the Bible as "proof." Misreading the shocked silence, the media demon in the sound booth punched his instant replay button and when the crowd heard her lie again, waving that book for support, the standing-room-only crowd of archdemons, demons, monsters, brutes, chimeras, gargoyles and little devils screamed their approval.

Without waiting for the official tabulation, Satan lifted his glass to the image of the little old lady still frozen mid-lie on the wall-sized screen. "Maybe," he thought to himself, "women can also be great liars." Then immediately he shouted above the bedlam, "To the really great lies!" he bellowed, "and to the poor, dear liars who tell them believing sincerely that they are working for God when in fact, THEY ARE WORKING FOR US!"

A Visit to Sodom

"Grace, remember those who call God's Queer Children 'Sodomites' have missed the whole point of the story. In fact they are the real Sodomites, for they have made outcasts of God's Queer Children."

Paul

GRACE

St. Peter led Grace to a park at the edge of the heavenly city. On a hilltop overlooking an endless expanse of green, two old men sat side-by-side on an iron bench reminiscing. For a moment, St. Peter stood listening to the ebb and flow of their animated conversation. Grace was amazed that two old men could speak so rapidly, often at the same time, while punctuating each phrase with a belly laugh or a loud groan, underlining each point with a passionate gesture.

"These are the two old saints God wants you to meet," Peter whispered to Grace, grinning to himself in anticipation of what would surely follow. "But child," he added, "getting their attention won't be easy. Even God had to use special effects to make these two stubborn souls pause long enough to listen." Then he added in a whisper, "The Creator had to use a burning bush to get that one's attention. The other one needed a blinding light from heaven."

The Old men in yarmulkes and shawls were completely oblivious to the angel who watched the debate flow back and forth between old adversaries who were also best of friends.

"Excuse me, Sirs," Grace said quietly.

The Old Ones didn't hear her or weren't interested in interrupting their heated conversation even long enough to try.

"Hello!" Grace repeated, this time louder and a bit perturbed.

The wrinkled, silver-haired man in the long beard and dusty robe looked down at the child for a moment and then continued arguing with his short, balding companion with the fierce eyes and strident gestures.

Finally Grace put her hands on her hips and yelled at the very top of her gruff little voice, "God sent us!" and immediately the noisy conversation died.

"Why didn't you say so?" long-beard asked, giving the little angel his full attention.

The short one looked up, noticed St. Peter and moved quickly to embrace him. "Peter," he said, "how long have you been standing there?" Then, spotting Peter's companion, a tough, pint-sized, and obviously very loud-mouthed angel, he added, "And what have we here?"

"This is Grace," St. Peter answered, "one of God's special envoys." And then to Grace he added, "And this rather intense old fellow is Moses, the 'Law Giver' and his loquacious friend, the Apostle Paul, once called Saul of Tarsus."

"Hello," Grace said bashfully, shocked that she was actually face-to-face with these two historic giants. Even Grace had heard the stories of Moses, the adopted son of an Egyptian Pharaoh, who had led the Jewish people out of slavery, and Paul, the founder of Christian churches across Asia.

"So, you are one of God's special envoys?" Paul asked, taking Grace by the hand and leading her to sit between them.

"Actually, she was appointed just this morning," Peter explained and then with a knowing smile, he added, "in the service of God's beloved Queer Children."

"Oh, dear," Moses said quietly, leaning back against the iron bench.

"Oh, dear. Oh, dear," Paul added, slumping down beside him.

Grace was confused at first and then angry. Her eyes flashed. She jumped to her feet and stood facing these two heavyweights.

"What's the matter with God's Queerfolk?" Grace asked defensively. "You have something against them?"

"No, no, no." Moses answered quickly. "It's not that we have something against them."

"It's what they have against us," Paul explained.

The two old men nodded in agreement.

"God's beloved Queer Children have something against you?" Grace asked. "How could that be?"

"It's something we wrote," Moses admitted, "over three thousand years ago."

"Two thousand years," Paul corrected. "Don't make me older than I am."

"What's a thousand years," Moses mumbled sadly, "to people who refuse to recognize the difference in what we wrote then and what it means now." Grace wasn't following their discussion.

"Child," Moses said softly, "at this very moment, people who take the Bible literally are misusing a handful of our verses to condemn God's Queerfolk."

"They are so busy misusing our words to support their own prejudice," Paul added, "that they don't take time to think about what our ancient truths really mean to their modern lives."

"Frankly," Moses said, "they're frightened of God's Queerfolk because they don't understand them and are corrupting our words to support their fear."

"But why do people fear them?" Grace asked.

"Because people are stupid," Paul said angrily. "And slow as snails to accept what seems 'different' or 'unnatural.'"

"You ought to know," Moses teased.

"Look who's talking," Paul replied and Peter had to interrupt to get these two old Jews back on track.

"For example," Moses began again, "religious leaders have misused my words for centuries to prove that women are inferior; to stone women caught in the act of adultery; and to favor the children of Sarah while they wage war against Hagar's offspring."

"And they've misused my words," Paul chimed in, "to drive lepers from our cities, to burn so-called witches and to keep women silent in the church."

"How's that working," Moses whispered grinning broadly but the Apostle would not be thrown.

"Now, out of fear and ignorance," he continued, "they are misusing our words to condemn God's beloved Queer Children. As a result they are rejected at home, driven from their synagogues and churches, humiliated in the streets, tried unfairly, imprisoned, castrated, hanged, beheaded, and burned at the stake."

Grace was confused and rather angry. "Why?" Grace asked. For a moment the two old patriarchs said nothing then Paul looked at Moses. "Tell us the story, old friend."

"He's a great story teller," Paul whispered to Grace.

"You're not so bad yourself," Moses replied.

"Actually," Paul answered, "I prefer writing letters, but you, Moses, when you tell a story bushes burst into flame, rocks spout water and the Red Sea parts. Youre stories are amazing, friend, even when they're true."

Moses placed his staff on the ground and sat down on the iron bench beside the feisty little angel-in-training. "Grace," he began. "All this confusion about God's Queerfolk began more than 3,000 years ago in the City of Sodom at the southwestern tip of the Dead Sea."

"That's why people call them Sodomites," Paul interjected.

"This is my story, Paul," Moses replied. "Are you going to let me tell it?"

Within seconds the news had spread across the heavens. Moses, revered by Christian, Jew and Muslim alike, was about to tell one of his unforgettable stories. Before he could even begin, the woods were filling up with angels and archangels leaning against the trees, sitting in the grass, crowding around the iron bench, straining to hear the first words of Moses' story.

Moses' sister, Miriam, arrived, kissed her elder brother on the cheek and sat down in the grass at his feet. At the last minute, the crowd made room in the front row for the prophet Isaiah who had been strolling through the garden with Ezekiel and Jeremiah. Everyone was rather stunned that in this illustrious company, one small, rather unimpressive angel seemed to be the center of attention.

Moses cleared his throat loudly and the crowd grew silent. He took a large parchment from the pocket of his robe and laid it at Grace's feet.

"This is Genesis," he said, "from the Torah: The first five books of the Jewish Law."

"He wrote them," Paul said grinning up at his friend. "And they're still best sellers."

Moses ignored Paul's remark, untied the cord, and unrolled the scroll to the middle of Genesis.

"The story of Sodom," he read. "This is where the trouble begins. That ancient city was a sinful place but Sodom's wickedness and its destruction had nothing whatsoever to do with God's Queer Children."

Grace was feeling somewhat distracted by the crowd. So she closed her eyes and focused on the words of Moses. In her imagination the great green meadow in this long lost garden became a hot and arid desert. The nearby rocks were transformed into the walls of Sodom, a near-Eastern city of at least a quarter-of-a-million inhabitants near the southern tip of the Dead Sea.

"God destroyed Sodom with fire and brimstone," Moses said, "and now it lies buried in sand beneath the shallow waters of the Sea."

"But what did the people of Sodom do?" Grace asked. "What made our loving Creator so angry that he would destroy an entire city?"

"Good question, Grace," Paul said. "Answer it correctly and you will discover exactly why the story of Sodom is not about God's Queerfolk."

"Paul!" Moses exclaimed.

"Sorry, old friend," Paul replied feeling somewhat foolish.

For a moment Grace thought she was imagining Sodom as Moses continued his sad account. Then she realized it was not her imagination. In some inexplicable, holy-graphical way she found herself standing next to Moses at the actual gates of that tragic city. The desert sun was setting. A cold wind began to blow. The roar of a distant, hungry beast frightened Grace. A beggar woman and her child sat nearby, hungry and cold. Around her lay dozens of outcasts, sick and dying, crying out for mercy. Grace saw a gang of thugs lurking in the shadows intent on mischief or worse. She grabbed Moses' hand. Together they walked quickly towards the gates of Sodom. The thick, wooden gates were closing as they rushed to get inside. Guards moved quickly to block their way.

"We are travelers from a distant land," Moses said quietly. "We need food, water and a safe place to spend the night."

The soldiers laughed and pushed away these strangers at the gate. But in the confusion, Grace saw two tall men dressed in desert robes step out of the crowd and into the city without being noticed by the guards. Grace recognized the strangers. They were angels. She had seen them at the Council of Elders. Why were they disguised as travelers from the desert? When the gates slammed shut, Grace pressed her face into a large crack between the wooden planks.

Inside Sodom she could see great marble fountains surrounded by two and three story houses ablaze with burning torches. Slaves rushed about preparing the evening meal. They carried trays loaded down with food and wine. The city smelled of expensive perfumes, exotic spices, fresh baked bread and lamb slow-cooking in olive oil over open kitchen fires. Guards patrolled the streets. Grace could hear laughter and music and the sound of happy voices.

"Sodom was an oasis in the desert," Moses explained, "rich, self-centered and doomed to destruction."

At that moment, a guard noticed the two distinguished foreigners standing alone in the shadows.

"You are strangers," he shouted. "How did you get in here?"

"Strangers!" a child yelled as he ran towards home sounding the alarm. An angry crowd began to gather. Sodom was rich but the Sodomites refused to share their riches. They built high walls and heavy gates to protect home and family. They hired armed guards to keep out anyone who did not belong. It didn't matter that the poor people left outside the city gates would face suffering, injury and even death in the night. Sodomites cared only about themselves and the preservation of their precious oasis in the desert.

As Moses spoke, Grace shared the terror felt by those who had been locked out, left to the mercy of the wild. The sick and dying, many with a terrible skin disease, moved towards them, more grotesque in the darkness than in the light, hands outstretched, brushing against them, begging for help. She could hear the growling of hungry beasts closing in on them. A starving baby in her mother's arms cried out in hunger and in pain. The frightened mother trembled from desperation and from the terrible cold that surprised desert travelers when the sun drops below the horizon. A gang of thieves approached in the shadows, whispering, encircling them, holding knives and pointed staffs.

"That's enough, Moses," Paul said interrupting the story. "Can't you see we're all shaking in our sandals?" Then he laughed and put his arm around Grace whose eyes were wide with fear.

"I'm sorry, child," Moses said, patting Grace on the knee with his wrinkled hand. "But to understand the real reason God condemned Sodom, you must feel the terror of those left outside the gate as well as the terror of strangers who were caught inside."

Grace pictured the angry crowd of Sodomites gathering around the foreigners, calling them names and threatening them with knives and swords. Then she noticed a middle-aged man pushing his way through the crowd. Thinking them some kind of royalty, he bowed before the two angelic strangers, offered dinner in his home and a guest room for the night.

"Behold, my lords," he said, "follow me quickly, rise early and go your way."

"No," they answered, "we will stay here in the street all night."

"Who is that good man?" Grace asked.

"He is Lot," Paul whispered, "Abraham's nephew. He has just moved into Sodom with his wife and daughters to invest and protect his fortune. And though Lot is rich, he is a newcomer to Sodom and not trusted by his neighbors."

"And who are the two strangers?" Grace asked.

"They are angels disguised as travelers," Moses replied.

"I knew it," she replied.

"Sent by God," Moses continued loudly, "to warn Lot that Sodom was about to be destroyed."

As Grace watched, a crowd of angry Sodomites formed to drive the angelic visitors from their city. By the time Lot convinced the strangers to enter his home the crowd had become a mob. All through dinner, the men and boys of Sodom continued to gather outside Lot's house, demanding "to know" the two strangers.

"They wanted what?" Grace asked surprised.

"You wrote it, Moses." Paul said. "What did it mean to you that the people of Sodom wanted 'to know' the strangers?"

"In ancient times, soldiers used sexual assault to punish a vanquished army," Moses explained looking a bit embarrassed as Grace struggled to take it in. "They raped the women, slaughtered the children, and sexually assaulted their helpless male captives to further humiliate them."

"Even now it's common down there on earth for one person to thrust his center finger into the air as a gesture of anger or defiance. It means, 'Rape you.' You'll even hear others say angrily, 'Up yours!' or 'Screw you!' another way of repeating the ancient threat. People forget that the gesture and the threats are both rooted in antiquity."

Quickly Moses continued the story. "Apparently the rape-your-enemy-to-humiliate-him tradition got hold of the men and boys of

Sodom. When they demanded that Lot send out the strangers Lot offered his own daughters in their place."

"Now that's disgusting," Grace interrupted. "I don't believe any father would do that."

"Fortunately," Moses said loudly, "when the men and boys of Sodom tried to break into Lot's home, the angels blinded them and led Lot, his wife and two daughters from the city.

"But what does the story of Sodom have to do with God's Queer Children?" Grace asked.

"Sodom's destruction had nothing to do with God's Queer Ones," Moses replied. "I wrote the story. I ought to know what it means."

"Careful friend," Paul teased, "remember your blood pressure."

Moses seemed irritated by Paul's remark but continued without a break.

"Unfortunately," he said, "more than one thousand years after I wrote that story in the Torah, Josephus, a Jewish historian living in Rome, decided that Sodom was about sex and the world has been confused ever since."

"Josephus was a Greek scholar," Paul added. "He was fascinated by the culture and values of ancient Greece. In translating the story of Sodom from Hebrew into Greek Josephus reflected the values of Greece and Rome and not the values of the Torah or the traditions of our people."

"To adapt the story of Sodom to fit the times," Moses continued, "Josephus implied that God destroyed Sodom because the men and boys of that city were all homosexuals. It doesn't take a scholar to know that all the men and boys in a city of at least a quarter-of-a-million people were NOT all homosexuals."

"The men of Sodom, both old and young, all the men from every quarter, surrounded the house," Paul quoted from Genesis 19:4 to help support Moses' point. Moses ignored the interruption.

"It doesn't take an historian to understand," he continued, "that the angry mob was intent on gang-rape to punish the strangers. And even the least informed know that God's Queer Children disapprove of gang-rape as much as God's Straight Children."

Moses ended his story. One by one, the crowd of angels and arch-angels left the grassy meadow. And though almost everyone had gone, Grace still sat on the iron bench between Paul and Moses, trying to understand exactly how the truth about Sodom would assist in her earth-mission to rescue and renew God's Queer Ones.

"It's really quite simple," Moses said. "Just tell the story as it happened. Fire and brimstone fell on Sodom because Sodomites valued wealth above all else and then refused to share it with the hungry, the homeless and the helpless. When they closed those gates to protect their wealth, they were breaking the heart of God and bringing down upon their heads the wrath of heaven."

Moses paused and looked towards Paul to see if his old friend had anything to add. Paul knelt down in front of Grace and began to speak.

"Those who call God's Queer Children sodomites are sodomites themselves," he said. "When they close the doors of their homes or churches and make outcasts of God's Queer Children, they too are breaking God's heart and risking the wrath of heaven."

At last Grace understood, or at least she thought she understood. She felt grateful for her time with these two great spirits but had no idea how to thank them. Finally, she simply walked over to Moses, stood on her tip toes and kissed him on the cheek. Then she turned to Paul, stretched to her full height and kissed his cheek as well. Then Grace took Peter's hand and together they walked towards the gates of the forgotten garden.

A Tour through Hell's Basement

"Up there, on earth about the same time Queers and other outcasts were dying in the gas chambers designed especially for the Jews, Americans also were torturing God's Queer Children in ways that warm old Satan's heart."

Satan

DEMION

At the very mention of the so-called "Sacred Writings" Satan began to laugh. The searing sound of Satan's snorts and snickers set off sirens across the underworld. The Devil's laughter was so shrill and so strident that the little demons in Queer Bashing 101 cringed and pressed their scaly fingers into their pointy little ears. Then suddenly, Satan stopped laughing.

"Follow me," he ordered with an evil twinkle in his blood-shot eyes. And without speaking a word he led the little devils into the dark and dingy basements of hell. The squad of demons who maintain that hideous, sprawling space are never told exactly when His Ugliness might appear. They were not surprised, therefore, when he arrived that night with the Archdemon and his class in tow.

The loud banging at the basement door alerted them to Satan's unannounced presence. Their Master never could remember the correct numbers on the combination lock, so he kicked at the door with his cloven foot and butted it with his hard, horned head.

"Open the damn door!" Satan shouted. The surprised and frightened door devils inside were still rolling out the fireproof red carpet and lighting the inner torches when the door crashed open.

"Welcome to R. & D.," Satan said gleefully to the students as they rushed through the barely opened doorway. "Hurry along now," he added leading them through the hot, glowing corridors, his grotesque shadow leaping ahead of them from wall to wall.

Summoned from his sleeping chamber just above the main archives, the Docent Demon who supervised hell's basement rushed after Satan's little party, muttering to himself, buttoning his red asbestos robe and fumbling with a mass of iron keys on a large brass ring.

"Unlock the castle," Satan ordered and the devils-in-training stepped aside to let the Docent Demon pass.

"You're going to love this place," Satan promised with a grin and a hideous giggle.

Demion led the sycophant students in an enthusiastic round of applause. They clustered around the Prince of Darkness, whispering to themselves while their professor, the Archdemon, tried to shush them into silence.

"Follow me," Satan bellowed as the Docent Demon finally managed to shoulder aside the heavy plank door and brush away the sticky tangle of cobwebs and bat droppings. "Now you'll understand the power of homo-phobia," he muttered proudly, sliding to a stop in the middle of a huge medieval fortress-like room built of massive stones with slit windows secured by iron bars. Pictures of esteemed barons, bishops and brigands lined the walls. Instruments of torture, carefully labeled and dated, were stacked neatly on display.

"I never dreamed that 'Queer fear' would infect the earth like a plague," Satan sneered. "Just because they are 'different,' every generation finds new ways to torture them. And," he added with glowing pride, "people are still misusing the Writings to justify torturing God's Queer Children."

At the name of God, the students giggled and guffawed, bowing and curtsying in mock homage.

"It was a lot more fun torturing the Queer ones in less civilized times," Satan confessed, "when our accomplices weren't so damned self-righteous." For a moment, Satan stood quietly in the center of that ancient torture chamber remembering the bad old days and hoping for their return.

"Their ancient plan was simple," he explained walking slowly towards a small iron door in the great rock wall. "When they caught

God's Queer Children making love, holding hands, or even smiling at each other across a crowded room, they were dragged through the streets past jeering crowds to the castle of a powerful baron, or to the cathedral of a 'holy' bishop. Deep in the basements or high in the towers there were cells like this one where God's Queer Children were locked in with the rats, the darkness and the bleached, white bones of those who came before."

"Is that all?" Demion asked, surprised and somewhat disappointed.

"Why you nasty little devil," Satan said affectionately, cuffing Demion about the ears. "Of course that wasn't all. The soldiers and the priests made them suffer in a million different ways. In fact," he added, leading the little demons back out of the cell into the flickering darkness of the central chamber, "in this very room you will see the prototypes for every breathtaking instrument of torture used on the Queer ones by our medieval friends."

"This is the rack," Satan purred as he caressed a huge, iron frame and the blood-stained leather straps that secured each prisoner into place. "I invented this one especially for the Inquisition."

"You invented it?" mumbled the Docent Demon, who knew the history of each basement room like the wrinkles on his bony hand.

"All right, they invented it," Satan whined, knocking the Docent Demon across the room with his hard red fist. "We just store their prototypes here. Actually," he whispered confidentially, motioning Demion and the other students to follow. "Our human friends don't need help when it comes to devising new ways to do evil, let alone torture God's Queer Children. But as a kind of favor to them, I take all the credit down here for what they do on their own up there."

Satan moved them quickly into the next room. Torches illuminated long red banners with black Nazi swastikas hanging from the ceiling. Satan walked proudly past display cases filled with leather whips, sharp knives, and armbands featuring yellow stars of David, badges of many colors and a pile of pink triangles. He flung open a second heavy door and led them into a huge prison chamber with a few barred windows, open toilets and floor to ceiling wooden planks for sleeping. The little demons climbed up on the bunks and made themselves comfortable.

"Less than a century ago," Satan began, "in Adolph Hitler's wretched little Reich, the Nazis invented the lie that they were a superior race." He paused, grinned, motioned for all the little devils to gather round, took a deep breath and whispered, "Anyone not born Aryan was an enemy of their 'master race' especially Jews, Gypsies, homosexuals, the physically and emotionally disabled, ethnic Poles, and Russians. Even old people were condemned just because they were different." The Devil repeated his favorite lie with such malice that the demons first gasped then applauded.

"That lie," Satan bragged, "spread across Europe and in a very short time millions of 'outcasts' and all sorts of political and religious trouble makers ended up in prisons like this one crowded onto these same bunks where you're sitting."

"But were the Queers imprisoned here?" Demion asked, thinking Satan had wandered off the subject.

Tired of being interrupted even by the Archdemon's protégé, Satan hurled one of his fiery pocket-size missiles in Demion's direction.

"Of course the Queers were imprisoned here," Satan shouted angrily. "Because they, too, were different, they ended up in Nazi concentration camps with millions of Jews and other victims of the lie."

Then he stared into the eyes of Demion and added, "Listen, you little devil, just because you're being trained in Queer bashing don't forget that anyone can use the lie. To whisper 'they are different' has the power to wreck a family or launch a world war. Hitler and his goose-stepping stooges whispered 'they are different' and millions of Jews and other innocent people including God's Queer ones were murdered in ways so hideous that even I was surprised at human ingenuity."

Satan was leading them down a long, white, sterile corridor in a fairly new addition to the basements of hell. They followed him into a medical waiting room, complete with magazines stacked on a coffee table and pictures of famous doctors and researchers hanging on the walls. At the Archdemon's cue, the little student devils took their seats while Satan whispered quietly to the Archdemon. Then Satan whirled to face them.

"Up there, on earth," he began, "about the same time Queers and other outcasts were dying in the gas chambers designed especially for the Jews, Americans also were torturing God's Queer Children in ways that warm old Satan's heart."

The Archdemon shivered with delight at what Satan had accomplished in his war against God's Queerfolk as recently as the 20th century. After Satan's first malicious whisper, "they are different," homophobia spread across the world like an airborne plague. Satan stopped his hideous laughter and continued.

"Priests and preachers used their pulpits to condemn God's Queer Children," Satan bragged. "Legislators passed laws enforced by the courts forbidding homo relationships. Police in many lands filled their prisons and high-walled sanitariums with 'inverts,' their more polite, scientific description of 'the different ones.' And doctors and psychologists researched new ways to eliminate 'the difference' altogether. They tried to 'cure homosexuals' through chemicals that caused nausea and vomiting, through testosterone or hormone injections, severe electric shock, lobotomies and even castration."

At this, even the little devils clutched their private parts and groaned. Satan didn't even pause. "Religious leaders invented their own 'cures,'" he added, "prayer and fasting, cold showers and behavior modification, counseling and celibacy, deprogramming camps, ex-gay therapies and homo-anonymous groups."

Suddenly Satan paused, looked around the room and added in a malevolent whisper of triumph, "AND BEST OF ALL," he concluded, "THEY'RE STILL DOING IT!"

Satan bowed with a flourish, expecting a standing ovation but the little demons continued walking behind him in silence. Suddenly, Satan understood their confusion.

"What's the matter, you little morons?" the Devil shouted angrily. "Don't you understand that no one can 'cure' homosexuality?"

Satan turned on the Archdemon. "Haven't you taught them anything?" Then whirling back to the demons-in-training he shouted. "Homosexuality isn't a sickness. The Creator never intended for it to be 'cured.' So it's your job to convince doctors and counselors, priests and pastors, friends and family that the Queer ones can and must be 'cured.'"

After a pause to catch his foul breath, Satan remembered one last "cure" he had almost forgotten. "Of course," Satan added proudly, "we must not forget the bullies, my precious little bullies who want 'to cure' the homos their way." Satan guided them to a display marked: "CURRENT!"

Satan loved bullies, his little "demons in the flesh." He pointed out a display of spray cans used for painting sodomite and faggot on walls and fences, the baseball bats studded with nails, the ropes, switchblades, and brass knuckles, the handguns and the rifles. There were pictures from police files taken at the scenes of crimes committed by bullies against God's Queer Children. Gloating with pride, Satan pointed to the ghastly police photos of the Creator's homofolk who had been tortured, beaten and murdered just because they were "different."

In the conference room in the basement of hell, the little demons sat staring at the photos, impressed by the power of Satan's lie. And though Satan was the first to whisper that lie, over the centuries it had taken a life of its own until millions of innocent men and women were dead.

"Well?" Satan said, looking down on his little demons, "What have you learned today?"

At that moment Demion understood what he was called to do, a calling shared by all his demon friends, their life's vocation. Satan saw the answer dawn in Demion's eyes.

"Demion?" Satan said quietly and his favorite little devil answered on cue.

"This is what I've learned, Master," he said. "Your lie that homosexuals need to be 'cured' is the reason God's Queer Children suffer and die and it's our job to keep your lie alive."

The Devil smiled, took Demion in his arms, and hugged him until the little demon gasped for breath.

"Keep the lie alive," Satan whispered and that whisper echoed up and down hell's basement.

At that moment the Docent Demon appeared carrying a tray of drinks for Satan and his late-night guests.

"Keep the lie alive," Satan jeered triumphantly, lifting a crystal goblet and holding it high overhead.

"Keep the lie alive," the Archdemon and his class echoed the toast. Then, as one, they gulped down their fresh hot toddies and tossed their glasses into the massive fireplace where the crystal shattered with the sound that wind chimes make as a sudden gust of wind blows them to the ground."

The Princess and the Saint

"Whenever I see the Light shining at the right hand of God, I remember an old friend and how brightly the Light shined in him and how in spite of my failures he caused the Light to shine in me."

St. Peter

GRACE

"Here we are," Peter said softly as they began the long, steep walk up the marble stairway to the great Cathedral of the Saints and Martyrs that towered above the Pearly Gates. "But, St. Peter ..." Grace mumbled, gripping his hand even more tightly as the carved bronze doors began to open and the sound of ten thousand voices echoed all around them singing a hymn of praise.

Angels, especially young ones, don't usually worship their Creator in the Cathedral. In fact, the huge heavenly edifice had been constructed rather recently (at least as eternity goes) for saints and martyrs arriving from Europe and North America who weren't comfortable worshipping in the open air.

Grace had toured the Cathedral campus during her school days as a cherub, but one glimpse inside that shadowy basilica echoing with murmured voices had sent her bolting for "the Green" where saints and martyrs from Africa, Asia, and South America sang and prayed in the open. Her adjunct professor in worship, a rather ancient English saint, had explained to Grace that Cathedral worship around the Prayer Book with all pomp and tradition was "rather an acquired taste" and that one day even she would feel at home in the Cathedral. But Grace had never understood why the Old Ones liked to sit on hard pews reading endless prayers when you could sing and dance your praises on "the Green."

"Take a deep breath, child," St. Peter said, leading her through the high arched doorway. "You'll be fine." He remembered how this normally tough little angel hated crowds especially in dark, shadowy places. He squeezed her hand and continued up the stairs.

"Before you begin your special assignment," he said, as they walked across the labyrinth and passed the fountain at the entrance of the Cathedral, "there are two more people God wants you to meet. We can usually find them here."

Reluctantly, Grace followed St. Peter through the carved, wooden doorway and across the narthex into the semi-darkness of the Cathedral nave. Sunlight streaming through stained glass windows pierced clouds of incense with streaks of emerald green and cobalt blue. Brightly colored banners hung from marble pillars fluttering gently in parade above the mass of saints and martyrs who knelt before the high altar where God sat on a golden throne surrounded by an angelic host.

For a moment Grace stood in awkward silence staring at the saints and martyrs seated nearby. Their eyes were filled with tears of joy. Their arms were outstretched in praise. Their tongues moved in silent songs of adoration. She looked up again at God on the high throne and noticed the bright white light burning nearby like an intense phosphorus-fed flame.

"What is that light at God's right hand?" Grace whispered.

For a moment Peter paused, trying to find the best way to describe the radiant presence that filled the front of the Cathedral with light.

"He is Truth," St. Peter replied, "and Love," he added "and Justice." For a moment St. Peter stood in silence staring into the Light. "It is the Son," he concluded and Grace could see that St. Peter was deeply moved as he looked into the Light.

"Are you about to cry?" she asked, looking into the eyes of her friend and squeezing his hand tenderly.

"It is the Light," Peter answered simply. "Whenever I see it, I remember an old friend and how brightly the Light shined in him and how in spite of my failures he caused the Light to shine in me."

Moved by his personal memories of the Light shining in darkness that could not put it out, St. Peter knelt on the marble floor. Like the saints and martyrs that filled that giant space, Peter, too, lifted his arms in praise. Like them, his lips began to move in some silent song of adoration. His eyes, too, filled with tears of joy and gratitude as he looked deeply into the Light and remembered his friend in whose life the Light had burned so brightly.

At that moment, God stood to bless the assembly. After the choral response echoed from the high altar to every corner of the nave, God and the entire entourage of angels disappeared. Herald trumpets played a final fanfare from somewhere high in the atrium. The Old Ones rose to their feet applauding. Peter stood, grasped Grace's hand, and led her into an alcove where she could see the Old Ones pass. The rush of music that flowed from a thousand silver pipes made her scalp tingle. When ten thousand voices joined in a hallelujah chorus of praise, a tear surprised that tough little angel as it appeared unbidden and drifted slowly down her cheek.

Grace watched as the aisles filled with saints and martyrs shaking hands, whispering "peace be unto you," and embracing old friends. Although she remained half-hidden in the shadows of a marble sculpture, Grace did notice the faces of the Old Ones as they passed by.

These were the kindest, strongest faces she had ever seen, but they were creased with lines of suffering and grief. Although they came from different centuries and religious traditions, although they recognized God by many different names, they had loved their Creator and served God faithfully. They shared a common commitment to the Spirit of truth and love and justice. They had refused to compromise with evil and as a consequence of their faithfulness they had suffered humiliation, torture, imprisonment, and even death.

Tough little Grace felt a kind of terror in the presence of so many noisy Old Ones. Peter was busy greeting friends and didn't notice his charge trembling slightly in the shadows. There were as many women as men in the crowd of saints and martyrs, maybe more. And at that very moment, two of those women, recent arrivals themselves, noticed the tough little angel still in her Heavenly Maintenance uniform peeking out at the passing crowd, obviously feeling awkward and out of place. The two women looked at each other and without saying a word moved together towards Grace.

At the last minute, she noticed the two women walking in her direction. Although these special souls seemed to have come from two very different worlds, she could tell that they loved each other dearly. One wore a nun's white sari with three bright blue stripes. Her back was slightly stooped. Grace could tell that she was very old by human standards and rather fragile with wrinkled, leathery skin. Grace noticed, too, that the old woman glowed with that same Light she had seen at the right hand of God. As the Old One approached, Grace noticed that she was leaning heavily on the strong, slender arm of a rather regal and extremely beautiful young woman, with short blond hair, still wearing a fashionable pant suit as though she had been called to heaven suddenly, without warning, from an evening in Paris. The two women stood arm-in-arm for a moment looking down at Grace still trembling in the shadows but when the old woman smiled Grace no longer felt afraid.

At that moment the very pretty young woman knelt before Grace, touched her freckled cheek and said softly, "My name is Diana. What's yours?"

"I am Grace," the angel replied, taking a deep breath and standing as tall as she could stretch, "and I have just been appointed to be one of the guardians of God's Queer Children."

Diana looked surprised. She managed to maintain that wonderful smile, but for a moment she looked terribly sad.

"So," she said quietly, "I'm meeting my replacement. Now you will love God's Queerfolk as I loved them."Grace looked confused.

"God's Queer Children, as you call them, are very special to me, too," the young woman began, "especially those who carry the HIV virus or those who live with AIDS. So often, they suffer and even die alone."

The little angel knew nothing of disease or of the physical and emotional suffering that goes almost automatically with that particular virus. But Grace knew in her heart that meeting these two special women was no accident and that she was about to learn something important.

"What should I do," Grace asked, "when I find one of God's Queer Children suffering or dying alone?"

Diana looked away from Grace up into the eyes of the old woman standing beside her in the stained white sari. She had taught Diana the lesson that had changed her life and given her such power. Diana smiled gratefully at the old woman, and the old woman smiled back. Then, Diana turned to Grace and spoke softly.

"Just reach out your hand and touch them," she said, and the look of tenderness in her eyes made Grace want to cry.

"Just touch them," the Old One repeated softly, "and God will do the rest."

All of a sudden, Grace found herself in the arms of that beautiful young woman. She had never been hugged before, not like this and she longed for Diana's strong hug to last forever. All too quickly Diana stepped back, looked down at Grace, and said quietly, "I hope that God's Queer Children bring the same kind of joy into your life that they brought into mine." Then, with a wink and another unforgettable smile, Diana and the Old One disappeared arm-in-arm into the parting crowd.

The organ recessional ended in another burst of antiphonal trumpets. The handful of saints and martyrs who had waited to hear the final triumphant chords echo in the almost empty sanctuary applauded gratefully and stood to leave. At that moment, Grace saw St. Peter walking quickly in her direction.

"It's time to go, Grace," he said quietly, respecting the vast silence of the empty cathedral.

"Where are we going now?" she whispered back.

"In God's time you will know," Peter replied, taking her hand. "In God's time ..."

A Field Trip to the Valley of Condemning Voices

"People must never learn that misusing their Holy Book to support evil began as one of my best ideas. Now misusing it has become a Christian tradition, especially by those who take it literally."

Satan

DEMION

The old yellow bus, leased from S.T.S. (Sheol Transport Services), coughed and lurched its way across the Beelzebub Memorial Bridge screeching to a stop at a scenic overlook high above the Valley of Condemning Voices.

"Everybody out," the Archdemon ordered as Demion and his classmates from Queer Bashing: 101 pushed out the emergency windows and clambered noisily down the sides of their bruised and battered bus to the boiling hot tarmac below. The little devils were so busy singing the 666th chorus of "Bottles of Blood on the Wall" that no one heard the condemning voices echoing up from the valley.

"Line up, you little devils," the Professor shouted. "This is a field trip, not a holiday."

The class groaned. Every evil spirit in hell, from the lowest demon to the Devil, himself, loves a human holiday. Christmas, Hanukah, Kwanza, and Thanksgiving are especially popular with the Devil and his henchfolk. On those special occasions all leaves are canceled and even the least of the demonic hoard is assigned surface duty to taunt and torment human families gathered around their decorated trees or festive tables, unaware that they are entertaining unseen guests who specialize in discord and division.

Because these invisible visitors know just how to work a room, what begins as a celebration often ends with some poor, unsuspecting soul rushing from the table in tears or slamming the door and driving away in anger and frustration. Because family members don't know how to recognize, let alone deal with the holiday demons in their midst, these meant-to-be-happy occasions often become "field days" for the Prince of Discord and his helpers.

"Line up and listen," the Archdemon hissed again as the horrid creatures straggled into formation.

Just as the last protesting demon stumbled into place, mischievous Demion yelled, "Potty break." Whooping and hollering with glee, all eighteen devils broke ranks again and rushed after their leader towards the public toilets nearby.

"Not so fast," the Archdemon sneered as he grabbed Demion by the ear with one scaly hand and slapped him hard across the face with the other.

Demion fell cringing to the tarmac. Always the brawler, the little devil tried to crawl away, bruising his knees and burning his hands on the hot tar. But the Archdemon, a fierce and feisty old fiend with flailing feet and fists, lashed out at his favorite student with a cloven hoof that sent the little devil hurdling across the parking lot head first into an iron barrel of tourist trash. Seeing Demion humiliated so painfully before his peers stopped the others in their tracks.

"That's better," the Archdemon declared as they stood trembling before him. "Now, shut up and listen."

At last the little devils grew quiet enough to hear the distant voices, loud, angry voices screeching to be heard. Without a word from their professor, the students rushed to the railing overlooking the Valley of Condemning Voices. The Archdemon smiled to himself and joined them.

Fires burned as far as the eye could see. Clouds of sooty black smoke cast a dismal pall across the valley. Men and women from every century were wandering through the gloomy haze, crying out words of condemnation, waving their Book and pointing their fingers in judgment, but no one was there to see or hear them.

That absence of an audience is the primary reason that the Valley of Condemning Voices is such a terrible penalty for those poor tortured souls. In hell, there is no one to read their "God hates fags" signs, no one to hear their voices condemning "the Gay lifestyle," no one to see their "protect family values" television specials. And so their condemning voices rise and fall for all eternity, unheard and unheeded.

"What are they saying?" Demion asked. "And what is that Book they're carrying?"

The Archdemon was pleased that his pet student had gotten to the bottom line so quickly. He moved to pat Demion on the head affectionately as a kind of "back in good graces" gesture, but the little devil ducked away, dreading another painful blow.

"They're talking about God," the old fiend explained and immediately the students hissed in unison, the loud, familiar hiss always heard when the Creator's name is mentioned. "And they call the book they're carrying the Word of God." Again the demons hissed.

"These condemning voices love to quote the Writings," the Archdemon continued, "and the wonderful part is they almost always get it wrong."

The Archdemon giggled to himself at the irony. Those who were supposed to know the Bible best almost always got it wrong. Then he stopped, leaned down until he was nose to nose with Demion and whispered confidentially.

"It's good they get it wrong," he muttered, "because if they ever get it right, we're doomed."

Demion looked confused.

Smack! The Archdemon hit him across the knuckles once again.

"Do I have to explain everything?" the professor yelled, then immediately lowered his voice to a whisper.

"They just can't seem to understand that the Book they're quoting is the story of God at work saving the world, not condemning it. It's a love story."

The demons groaned.

"But fortunately for us," the Archdemon continued, "they get it all wrong. They misuse God's love story in ways that feel like hate to God's Queer Children."

The demons hissed, then hissed again.

"Now," their teacher continued, "it is your job to make sure they continue to get it wrong because getting it wrong leads to sorrow and bloodshed and death, oh my!"

Demion and his demon friends repeated the chant they had learned in basic training: "Sorrow and bloodshed and death, oh my!"

Suddenly Satan appeared in a flash of lightning, a peal of thunder and a cloud of dark black smoke. The Archdemon and his class scattered at his unexpected appearance. Satan loves to make a dramatic entrance. He laughed at their terrified response and began their favorite chorus in a voice that echoed across the Valley:

I'm the Devil. You're the dead.
You hoped for heaven. It's hell instead.
Here you'll suffer. Here you'll cry.
Sorrow and bloodshed and death, oh my!

Satan motioned for them to join him on the line they loved best: "Sorrow and bloodshed and death, oh my!" The demons obeyed happily. As they repeated the Devil's words thousands of other demons picked up the chant until it echoed across the Valley of Condemning Voices and even to the world above.

When Satan finally tired of his chant, he sat down on a stalagmite near a field of crosses and whistled for Demion and his classmates to gather 'round. The little devils collapsed in a semi-circle at Satan's feet. They were stunned to see him reach into a pocket and pull out a well-marked copy of the Bible. Seeing the terror in their eyes, the Devil thrust the Book towards Demion who screamed and tried to scramble away.

The demons laughed as Satan pulled Demion back into the circle. "You don't have to be afraid of the Bible if you misuse it carefully."

Demion and his classmates looked confused as Satan began to explain how they could misuse the Book in stealing the souls of God's Queer Children. Only Demion had the courage to interrupt.

"Whatdaya mean, use the Bible?" he asked waiting to be slapped or pummeled or kicked for asking.

"I said 'misuse' the Bible," Satan explained holding his anger in check. "I did not say 'use' it."

"All of it?" Demion asked taking his second big risk of the day and then trying to impress Satan he added quickly, "All 66 books; 1,189 chapters; and 31,102 verses?"

"Not the whole Bible," Satan shouted clenching his teeth and trying to be patient. "There are just six or seven brief verses that you can use to clobber God's Queer ones. You don't have to read the rest of it. Just memorize those six or seven verses and every time a Queer comes up for air, have his or her friends and family misuse those ugly little lines again."

"But what do they really mean?" Demion asked, scanning quickly the short lines used to condemn homosexuality and homosexuals.

"Never mind what those passages from the Book might have meant in their ancient times or in their original Hebrew or Greek," Satan shouted.

"Never mind that neither Jesus nor the Jewish prophets said anything against homosexuality or homosexuals.

"Never mind that the ancient authors were convinced that all people were heterosexual and anyone who acted differently was breaking the laws of nature.

"Never mind that these passages were translated into old English almost five hundred years ago by scholars working for a queer king.

"Never mind that there isn't a word for homosexual in either Greek or Hebrew.

"Never mind what scientists have discovered about sexual orientation and gender identity since the Book was written.

"Never mind the truth. That's God's problem," Satan screamed, spitting out the word and pausing just long enough for his students to hiss obediently. "Just do what you are told."

Satan jumped down off the stalagmite and began to walk slowly back and forth, the Bible in his hands. As he paced, he described how these writings had been misused to support bloody crusades and appalling inquisitions; to justify slavery, segregation, and apartheid; to persecute Jews and other non-Christian people of faith; to execute women as witches; to support Hitler's Third Reich and the Holocaust; to oppose scientific, medical, and psychological discoveries; to support the Ku Klux Klan; to condemn interracial marriage; to support child labor and the suffering and inequality of women. The list was endless and as he quoted from it Satan began to smile. When he finished the list of ways people have misused the Bible throughout history, he began to laugh so hard that everyone in hell could hear him laughing.

"Now, little demons," he said choking back his laugher, "that same book is being misused in the very same way to cause prejudice, fear and hatred against God's Lesbian, Gay, Bisexual, and Transgender creations.

"What in hell is a Transgender?" Demion muttered, adding the new word to his list of enemies.

"Never mind," Satan answered. "You'll find out along the way. Just remember that what people on earth call the 'T's' are the MOST vulnerable of all. Thanks to us, Transgender people suffer more discrimination, more intolerance and more hate crimes than all the others put together. Even their homosexual and bisexual sisters and brothers have a tendency to ignore and even avoid them.

Satan paused and then added, "But beware the 'T's'," he said. That 'T' also stands for tricky, tough and tenacious. At this moment the 'T's' are on the move. They've realized that justice and equality will never be given them. So they're rising up to take it for themselves. It's your job to stop them," Satan said and then added with a malicious grin. "Don't worry. You'll have plenty of help up there."

For a moment, the Devil paused, remembering Stonewall and the drag queens who helped launch a revolution. The thought of those troublesome queens in blue taffeta and three inch heels taking on "New York's finest" made his blood boil and his eyes flash red with anger.

"People must never learn that misusing the Holy Book to support evil began as one of my best ideas. Now misusing it has become a Christian tradition. Especially," he added confidentially, "by those who take it literally."

"Memorize those six little passages down here and carry them with you up there," he hissed. "Then whisper them into the ears of anyone who comes in contact with God's Queer Children. Repeat them, over and over again, until they take hold permanently in the minds and hearts of their pastors and priests, their parents, families and friends."

The Archdeacon smiled at the wit and wisdom of the Prince of Lies.

"If God's Queer Children hear those passages often enough," Satan continued, "they will begin to believe them. They will retreat deep into their closets, exactly where we want them, in the dark, alone, cut off from families and friends, isolated by guilt, traumatized by fear, dying to love and be loved, feeling lost, angry and without hope, convinced that even God doesn't love them."

The Poet of Lost Souls grew silent. The class was enthralled by Satan's sudden eloquence. No one had written a word in his notebook. Then, without thinking, Demion broke the silence.

"Those closets," he said quietly, "sound like hell to me." And even the Devil was stunned by Demion's sudden, unexpected brilliance.

XII

Grace at the Speed of Light

*"There is a quiet love song at the center of the universe.
When you are afraid, or you feel lonely or depressed, listen
for that song. It is the sound of the Creator humming to
Herself as she repairs and renews Creation."*

St. Peter

GRACE

"Here we are," St. Peter said softly as they approached a tall, stone tower in a thickly wooded grove at the edge of the campus. Grace stood at the mighty tower's base using her free hand to shield her eyes from the bright and flashing lights that darted in and out of a thousand open windows. When she squinted long and hard at the lights, Grace could see that they were angels, entering and exiting the tower at the speed of light. She was astonished at the sight. In her four difficult years on campus, Grace had never noticed the tall, brightly shining tower made of giant stones or the army of angels flashing about like hummingbirds in a field of wild flowers.

"Come in, child," said a voice that sounded so warm and welcoming that Grace almost burst into tears. The stories of earth-mothers had always fascinated her. When she turned to seek St. Peter's direction, he was gone. It was then Grace noticed the door that opened silently in the tower wall. A bright light shown from the doorway, like those bright, angelic lights she had seen moving in and out of the endless windows overhead. And though the light looked and felt like love itself, Grace was afraid to enter.

"Don't be afraid, little one," the voice spoke again, this time to the very heart of Grace, acknowledging her fear and, at the same time, ending it. Like the unwed teenage girl in Nazareth who heard that greeting almost two thousand years ago, Grace was no longer afraid. Suddenly, she wanted more than anything to enter the tall tower and throw herself into the arms of that mysterious presence.

In just a few short steps, Grace was inside. The interior of that rather formidable structure was unlike any heavenly residence she had ever seen. One great room stretched upward endlessly. It was brightly illuminated from the primary source of light above and from the lights that trailed behind each entering and exiting angel.

A wide wooden stairway clung to the inside of the tower wall, circling gently upward toward the light. And the smooth white walls of that great room were covered with portraits in gilded frames. Grace noticed that the paintings were of human faces, hundreds of thousands of them, and they all seemed to be looking upward toward the light.

A small platform or balcony had been built on the staircase beneath each open window. After rushing through the open space, the busy angels seemed to pause on those hand-carved wooden landings just long enough to stare intently at the paintings and then up at the light before darting away.

For a moment, Grace stood at the bottom of the stairway, watching the angels high above her. She was entranced by the flashing lights and the quiet, breezy undulation of a thousand angel wings. Just as she was beginning to wonder if she would ever fly that fast, Grace heard another sound from somewhere within the brilliant light, the sound of the same loving voice that had called out her name. Only now the voice was humming a beautiful, haunting melody, like a cello concerto, deep, and strong, and vibrant.

During her training as an apprentice cherub, Grace had heard St. Peter describe that same wondrous sound. "There is a quiet, confident love song at the center of the universe," Peter had explained. "When you are afraid, or you feel lonely or depressed, listen for that song. It is the sound of the Creator humming to Herself as She repairs and renews Creation."

Never before had Grace heard the love song. As she stood looking towards the light, listening to the humming of the Creator, Grace felt the tension just melt away. She could see that the angels, too, were comforted by the Creator's song. She noticed that just before flying away again, each angel would look upward just long enough to let the Creator's light and love song flow into them. A few of the angels knelt down to pray. Others just smiled up at the glorious light before disappearing in a flash out an open window. As Grace stood there staring upward towards the light, the loving presence spoke her name again.

"Come up the stairs, Grace," the voice said tenderly.

Grace squinted one last time into the light, hoping to see the heavenly being who had spoken. The voice was strangely familiar yet entirely unknown to her. When and where before had she heard her name spoken with such amazing love? Grace closed her eyes and tried to remember. The voice had been different and yet the same.

"Grace?"

Suddenly, Grace knew for certain where she had heard that voice. She rushed to the stairway and began to leap up the stairs two at a time, around and around the inside of the great, open tower. Surrounded by the busy angels and the endless portraits, Grace moved upward towards the light. The stairs went on forever and the pictures stretched upward and downward to infinity, but with every step, Grace drew closer to the heavenly being living and singing in the light.

Finally, the determined little angel stood at the top of the long, wooden stairway, doubled over with exhaustion and gasping for air. When she caught her breath and looked up again, Grace found herself blinded by the light that flowed from the corner of the splendid, glowing room at the very top of the tower.

"Come, Grace," said the familiar voice. "Come into the light."

"Abba," she said, recognizing the voice for certain, rushing into the bright unknown, sure that her Creator was waiting there. But inside the light, when Grace's eyes had adjusted to the light, the tough, little angel discovered to her blinking surprise that Abba had changed. No longer throwing lightning bolts or clapping up thunder, the Heavenly presence sitting before her was soft and gentle and holding out Her arms.

"I am your Mother, Grace," said the Creator, "as I am your Father. I have created you and I love you just as you are."

Grace moved quickly into the lap of God. She threw her arms around the Creator's neck and whispered, "I love you, too." For one, long, holy moment she lay in the breast of her Creator, feeling God's hands stroking her short, red hair and wiping away her joyful tears.

"Never forget how much I love you," said the voice, and just hearing the Creator's words gave Grace a sense of peace that she had never known. "I am loved by the Creator of the Universe," Grace thought to herself. "And I am loved just as I am." After an infinity of tenderness, Grace climbed down from the Creator's lap and knelt before Her.

"Mother-God," the little angel asked, stammering slightly from excitement, "why have you brought me here?"

"Look at the pictures, Grace," Her Creator said simply, "and you will know why."

Grace found herself being helped to her feet by the Creator. Together, they walked hand in hand through that gallery of human faces in gilded frames. At first, the little angel was too overwhelmed by God's loving presence to look closely at the pictures. She was, after all, walking hand in hand with the Mother of Creation. She did notice, however, that an angel stood at attention beside each gilded frame. The angels bowed deeply as their Creator walked by. Caught up in that magic moment, Grace moved among the portraits, seeing little and understanding less.

"Look more closely at the faces, Grace," God said kindly, but this time the distracted little angel understood it as a command.

Art was not high on her list of special interests. Grace never spent Saturdays wondering about heavenly galleries or museums. Instead, she loved to camp in the woods, to fish, and hike and climb. But she did like to study the human faces of the saints and martyrs when they walked past her on the golden streets and there was something special about these tower faces. So Grace obeyed her Creator and strained to look more closely at the faces in the gilded picture frames.

It was then she noticed that the human faces in those windows were not paintings. They were alive. Their eyes blinked and their lips moved. There were black faces and white. There were red, yellow and brown faces and their expressions changed even as Grace watched. There were old, wrinkled faces and the smooth-skinned faces of young people. They all seemed to be looking up towards the Creator and their lips were moving.

"They are praying," Grace whispered, startled by her own discovery, turning to face her heavenly Mother. "Praying to you?"

The Creator nodded slightly.

"Now, look at their eyes, Grace," She said, "and tell me what you see."

It didn't take long for Grace to notice that the eyes staring out at her were filled with pain.

"They are sad faces, Mother," Grace whispered.

Again, the Creator nodded. For a moment they walked in silence among the faces. Angels on duty bowed low as they passed.

"This level of the tower is used exclusively to frame the prayers of my Queer Children," the Creator said with such compassion in Her voice that Grace wanted to cry, "and they are sad because they think I do not love them exactly as they are."

The Creator paused to look more closely at the unhappy face of a young woman staring up at them. There were tears in her eyes and a rather desperate look on her face. Her lips were moving and the Creator bent down to listen.

"This is a Lesbian mother," God whispered. "A judge has taken away her young son because he believes that she is 'unfit' to be a parent."

As God listened to the Lesbian mother's prayers, Grace noticed that her Creator's face changed from that of loving parent, to resolute judge. When She spoke again, Her voice rang with God's eternal call to do justice.

"The decision to separate that child from his mother," God explained to Grace, "hinged entirely upon the judge's prejudice that Lesbians are not good mothers. It is not true. Throughout human history, my Lesbian Daughters and Gay Sons, my Bisexual and Transgender Children, all my Queerfolk have parented as lovingly and as well as my Heterosexual Children. Again, bigotry, not truth, has prevailed."

Grace watched closely as God's face changed again from judge to loving mother. The little angel could see how the suffering of Her innocent Lesbian daughter had touched God's heart. As She listened intently to the prayers of that anguished mother, the Creator reached out to wipe her tears away.

"I love you, child," She whispered, "and I have heard your prayers." Then, the Mother of Creation, that weeping Lesbian's own heavenly mother, turned to the angel that stood at attention by that sad face, and said, "Tell her that I love her and that I am with her always. Tell her now!"

Smiling proudly, the guardian angel reached up to touch the face of God, bowed low, and in a flash disappeared out the tower's open window. Grace was stunned by the sheer volume of love that had flowed at the speed of light from the Mother of the Universe into that waiting angel and then down toward the Lesbian mother on the earth below.

Grace continued looking into the eyes of that sad but beautiful Lesbian in the picture frame. No one moved. No one spoke. Then, Grace blinked in surprise. At that very instant, the Lesbian mother smiled as a child rushed into her arms. She held her son tightly and with tears of gratitude streaming down her face, she looked up once again into the eyes of God. The Creator smiled, squeezed the hand of Grace, and moved on.

"This is a young Gay sailor," the Creator said softly, stopping before the portrait of a handsome man in a naval uniform. For a moment, God leaned forward again to listen.

"He is a crewman on an American warship. Everyone knows that my Queer Children serve with courage and integrity in the armed forces of every nation. But a handful of this boy's shipmates have teased and tormented him for the entire cruise. One drunken sailor has threatened his life. My Gay child is afraid."

At that moment, the Creator reached out to touch the young sailor's face. Once again, She said those important words: "I love you, child. I love you exactly as you are." And once again, She turned to the angel on duty beside that gilded frame and whispered, "Tell him, now!"

That angel, too, reached out to touch the face of God. Then she bowed low and disappeared in a blaze of light. Once again, Grace took the hand of God and waited for the miracle of love to happen, this time to the Creator's homosexual son. Then, without warning, the handsome young face in the portrait looked back over his shoulder in terror. Other hands appeared in the gilded frame, bruising and beating God's child. His Creator groaned in agony and anger as the innocent sailor was attacked by drunken shipmates.

The vicious, unprovoked attack went on for several terrible minutes. Still trying to ward off the deadly blows, the Gay sailor turned again toward the face of God. Although blood was flowing down the young man's face and his eyes were already swelling shut, his lips moved one last time in prayer. Then his eyes closed and his face disappeared from view. At that moment, the Mother of Creation groaned with such grief and such anger that Grace fell to the floor in terror.

"I love you, child," God shouted out the nearby open window. "And I promise you that one day justice will triumph and the suffering of my beloved Queer Children will end. But until that day, my son, come home, come home to Mother, where there is no terror and your pain will be no more."

Still frightened by the sudden turn of events, Grace looked on with wonder as the angel God had assigned to the young Gay sailor flew in through the tower's open door. She was carrying a bright new, liberated soul in her arms.

"Welcome home, my child," the Creator said, leaning down over the wooden railing and reaching out Her arms in welcome. Her words were so warm and loving that they sent shivers up and down Grace's spine. In one voice, all the angels in the tower, thousands of them, echoed God's welcome. "Amen!" they shouted as the young man and his angelic escort began to ascend the long, curving stairway towards the light.

For a moment, every angel flew in place, honoring the presence of this new spirit in their midst. And the song those angels sang and the trumpets those angels played could be heard across the heavens. Every angel and archangel inside and outside the tower, every cherub and seraph, every saint and martyr in heaven stopped and bowed low to honor the arriving soul of one of God's Gay Children.

With Grace now at Her side, the Creator stood at the top of the stairway waiting to welcome home Her innocent child. When that Gay sailor finally reached his heavenly Mother, She took him in Her arms and held him close. As Grace looked on, God's tears mingled with the tears of the angels and flowed like a mighty, healing stream to the earth below.

When the celebration ended and the soul of the Gay sailor had been guided safely to his new, heavenly home, the Creator resumed Her slow, thoughtful walk among the gilded portraits, pausing here to touch a troubled face or there to whisper, "I love you, child. I love you exactly as you are." Once again, angels flew quickly in and out the open windows. And once again, the Creator sang Her song of love to all God's Queer Children in heaven and on the earth below.

Grace stood awkwardly in the shadows. She thought God had forgotten her and was about to sneak away down that long wooden stairway, when she was drawn mysteriously to an empty gilded frame hanging on the tower wall. Suddenly, a human face appeared in that frame, staring up at her. It was the face of a thirteen-year-old boy in a Boy Scout cap and uniform. His white face was tanned and freckled by the sun. From time to time, he looked back over his shoulder nervously. Matching Scout tents stretched toward the nearby woods. The boy seemed lonely, perplexed. His lips were moving, but Grace couldn't make out the words. His blue eyes blinked back tears.

As Grace stared at the boy in the gilded frame, the little angel's heart began to beat fast like the drum that St. Peter uses to summon cherubs to the athletic field. Frantically, she looked around for the Creator. She was far down the tower's stairway, touching the face of another of Her Queer Children, whispering words of comfort, commanding a host of busy angels.

Grace was getting nervous. The Boy Scout in the gilded frame seemed desperate. She leaned forward and strained to hear the young boy's prayer. Apparently, he had fallen in love with his tentmate, another thirteen-year-old Boy Scout. He felt guilty. He was confused and obviously afraid.

"Help me," the boy cried. "Take away these feelings, please," he said, over and over again. Grace felt the boy's urgent pain and she wanted to help but she had no idea where to begin.

"Help me," the boy prayed again, tears streaming down his face. "I don't want to feel this way. Help me change."

Grace knew she had to act, even though the Creator was still far away. With a spontaneous cry, Grace reached out to touch that sad, frightened face.

"God loves you, child," she whispered, trying to say the words exactly as her Creator had said them. "God loves you exactly as you are."

As Grace spoke that powerful promise, she began to tremble with feelings she had never known before. Her short, muscular body stretched upward toward the ceiling of heaven. Her wings filled out and began to oscillate with the speed and power of the wind. Her heart beat stronger and her spirit longed to fly.

"God loves you, exactly as you are," Grace shouted across the distance, and she knew that something wonderful was about to happen. At that very moment, or so she told me later, Grace felt the hand of God on her shoulder.

"Go tell him, Grace," that loving voice commanded simply. "Tell him now." Without even pausing to ask all the questions that were forming in her mind, Grace reached up slowly to touch the loving face of God before flying out the open window at the speed of light.

I thought it was a shooting star that streaked through the night sky above our Boy Scout camp in the thickly forested hills above my hometown. I was just thirteen, a young Gay man just beginning to wonder why I was different. That same night I had prayed that God would help me understand why I had such feelings about my tent mate. As he lay beside me I could hear him breathing. I wanted to touch his face, to kiss his cheek, to hold him. I lay awake all night feeling excited and afraid. "Please God," I prayed again and again, "take these feelings away."

I didn't learn until much later that those feelings were natural, God-given, as much a part of my life as breathing. I should have been thanking God for those feelings. Instead I thought God didn't care about me. In fact, God had heard my prayers and answered them, not by taking away those feelings but by sending Grace flying faster than the speed of light in my direction.

Demion Meets His Match
(July 17-1953)

*"Never forget, when you maim the soul of the boy, you
maim the soul of the man."*

The Prince of Lies

DEMION

In a rather garish, badly decorated executive suite occupying the
entire top floor of the highest building in Hell, the Prince of
Darkness was presiding over a late-night meeting of his various
department heads. Couriers, spies, personal aides and cringing toadies rushed in and out of the room. An assortment of autographed
"Thanks for your help..." pictures signed by political and religious
leaders from around the world were tacked to the hot, steaming wall
behind his tasteless gold and sequined throne.

Satan, known by his more intimate friends as "Bezel," lifted a
glass of cheap champagne to toast his latest victories in his battle
to steal souls. The archdemons and department heads cheered and
applauded wildly after Satan's surprise announcement that Transgender men and women had become the number one victim of hate crimes
in the U.S.

"To bigotry in the courtroom and blood in the streets," Satan
shouted as servants rushed to refill their empty glasses.

As drinks were downed and new bottles opened, Satan noticed
his Archdemon and the graduating class from Queer Bashing 101 —
The Adolescent Years standing in the waiting room.

"Ah, graduation exercises," the Evil One exclaimed. "I almost
forgot. Let the celebration begin."

To the stirring but rather worn-out sounds of Elgar's "Pomp and Circumstance" the graduates entered the room. The Archdemon, wearing full academic regalia, an ancient, awkward custom that Satan himself had invented to make graduates suffer, marched at the front of the class.

"Spirit of Evil," he intoned proudly when the class was fully assembled at Satan's feet, "I take great delight in presenting to you Demion, our Valedictorian, the nastiest little soul thief in the bunch, and his graduating classmates from Queer Bashing 101.

Satan smiled and stepped forward to shake young Demion's hand. After whispering words of congratulations that singed the wiry hairs in Demion's left ear, the Prince of Evil presented his meanest, most malevolent graduate a colorful diploma and a large, sealed envelope containing the photo and a complete background file on his first young homosexual victim on earth.

Demion rushed back to his seat and slit open the envelope with one, long, razor-sharp nail. As the class of gay-bashers continued to process across the stage, Demion grasped the 8x10 photo in his packet, squinted his beady red eyes to focus in the smoky, semi-darkness, and looked deep into the blue eyes of a thirteen-year-old Boy Scout.

"He's just a boy," Demion whispered, showing the photo to another demon who had just received his degree. "The best damn demon in the class and he assigns me a baby Queer to torment."

Much to Demion's embarrassed surprise, his loud, disappointed whisper echoed across the quiet room. Satan whirled angrily, charged through the waiting line of graduates, grabbed Demion by one long, pointy ear and lifted him high above the cheering crowd.

"Who's in charge here?" Satan shouted with such a roar that even the Archdemon ducked for cover.

"You are, Sir," Demion whimpered, dangling rather unceremoniously in the midst of the most important ceremony of the year.

"And you?" asked the Devil loudly, "Who are you?"

"I am your servant, Demion, demon-first-class," the poor devil gasped, his throat filled with smoke and his eyes watering from the poisonous fumes that rise continuously to the ceiling in every room in hell.

"And what is your duty?" the Devil roared, bouncing Demion up and down like a yo-yo while his fellow classmates grinned with glee at the embarrassing and rather painful plight of the classmate they most detested.

"To obey, Sir," Demion whispered, terrified that any moment the Devil might demote him permanently to that vast crowd of demons who failed Queer Bashing 101 and spent the rest of their eternity shoveling coal and stoking fires.

"Say again!" the Devil screamed, and demons across the kingdom shivered at the sound.

"To obey, Sir," Demion gasped, fearing this was the end of his short and rather mediocre academic career.

After suffering this very public humiliation, Demion found himself sprawled on the steaming floor of hell surrounded by his jeering friends. The once proud little demon was still lying there, coughing up smoke and struggling to focus, when the Prince of Darkness leaned down over him and spoke in a melodramatic stage whisper loud enough for all of them to hear.

"Just a boy?" Satan hissed like a cobra set to strike. "Just a boy?" he hissed again only this time Satan was the cobra, his hood extended, his forked tongue darting in and out, swaying just above the terrified demon. "Just a boy?" the demonic cobra hissed a third time as he struck directly at Demion's face.

The poor demon was still screaming when the snake vanished and Satan reappeared holding in his hand the picture of the thirteen-year-old Boy Scout Demion had been assigned. Satan held my photo just inches above Demion's unblinking eyes and whispered with such force that even the angels guarding the outer ramparts of heaven trembled at the sound.

"Never forget," he sneered, "when you maim the soul of the boy, you maim the soul of the man."

After waiting a few more seconds to be sure his clever little demonstration had made his point, the Devil began to laugh. The other demons picked up the laughter as the Prince of Darkness helped Demion to his feet, dusted him off and returned him to his classmates, laughter still echoing to the farthest corner of hell.

"Who's next?" Satan growled as the Archdemon rushed to get the graduates back in line. One by one every little demon from Queer Bashing 101 approached to receive a diploma, the envelope containing a first assignment and a hot, putrid kiss on both cheeks from the Chief Bogeyman himself. When the last little devil was honored, Satan walked to the first of all the "bully pulpits" and looked out across their bright red shining faces.

"This may seem like an ending," he said, trying to think back on all those interminable, human graduation speeches he had inspired, "but it is really only a beginning."

The graduating demons applauded wildly having been warned by the Archdemon that Satan, also nicknamed His Triteness, kept a record of every burst of applause and standing ovation he received just like Satan's secret friends up there, the preachers and politicians whose words soared to the heavens but whose souls were already half-way to hell.

"As you leave on your first assignment to steal the souls of God's Queer Children," Satan continued, "remember my final words to you."

The little devils sat up in their chairs, straining to hear the Master Soul Killer's advice.

"If you really want to steal the souls of God's Queer Children," Satan said quietly, "you don't have to misquote their holy book. You can trust their pastors, priests and Sunday school teachers to misuse those seven little verses against them. You don't have to call them 'faggots,' or 'fairies,' or 'dykes.' Their classmates and co-workers will do that for you. You don't have to make them feel condemned or abandoned or unloved. Their parents and friends are experts in that department. And you don't even have to lie about them, or whip up the nation into a violent, homophobic frenzy, or organize voters to eliminate their civil rights. I have special friends up there who are doing all that very effectively. But to steal the souls of God's Queer ones, there is one thing you must do without fail."

The Evil One paused behind his bully pulpit to sip from a glass of tepid water. The Archdemon smiled in anticipation of the Boss's grand finale. The little devils pulled pads and pencils from the pockets of their robes ready to write down every inspired word. Satan leaned forward and whispered confidentially.

"This is my own special secret," he said proudly and the whole underworld strained to hear. "To steal the souls of God's beloved Queer Children, you must make them believe they ought to change."

"Ought to change what?" one of the dumber demons whispered to the Archdemon.

"From Queer to straight, of course," the Archdemon whispered back, but the student demon still looked perplexed. "From homo to hetero," old Fury tried again only this time he whispered so loudly that even Satan stopped to listen. "From girly-boy to manly-man," the Archdemon shouted, "from diesel dyke to womanly woman, from Sodomite to Stud."

Satan liked where this was going and on the spot skipped to the finale of his graduation speech. "From Gay to ex-gay," he added to the list with a special sneer on the label "ex-gay," Satan's absolutely favorite deception.

"Above all else," he said again, "make them think they ought to change."

With those words, the Prince of Darkness began to laugh again.

"Why is he laughing this time?" the dumber demon asked.

"He is laughing," the Archdemon replied, "because he knows they cannot change and that they shouldn't even try."

Satan knew what happened in the lives of God's Queer ones when they were told by well-meaning pastors and parents that say (or just infer) that God couldn't really love them until they change.

"Make them think they ought to change," Satan repeated," and they will die trying."

With Satan's words still ringing in their ears, the Archdemon led Demion to the highest pinnacle in hell, hugged his favorite student warmly, and watched as the little devil thrust upwards at the speed of darkness through the earth's shifting tectonic plates.

Exploding with evil energy, pushing massive boulders aside, swimming through oil fields and underground lakes, Demion broke through the earth's fragile crust and stood shaking off the dust and grime in a moonlit.

It took only a moment for Demion's bright-red, evil eyes to focus on the Boy Scout camp in the forest clearing. Seconds later he spotted the open tent where I lay wide awake and miserable. Walking on the tips of his sharp little hooves, Demion sneaked across the camp, leaping from shadow to shadow, only partially hidden by the pools of darkness. As he advanced he was rehearsing the lies he had learned in hell, lies he was about to try out on me: "You are different! You must change!"

Demion was so eager to begin his Master's business, so preoccupied with rehearsing the Devil's lies, so intent on stealth that he didn't notice Grace already standing guard in the shadows near my tent. Just as he stooped down to enter, she tackled Demion from behind.

Years later, the little devil finally admitted that Grace pinned him to the earth that night and held him there in a hammer-lock, helpless and in pain. Of course Demion insists that the "angel brat" only held him down "for a few seconds or so." But Grace swears she could have held him pinned to the ground until the sun rose and the bugle sounded but she stopped and let him go because somewhere in the darkness she heard a familiar voice.

"Let him go, Grace," the Creator said firmly.

"But, Abba," the tough little angel replied, "we've got him now. Let's finish him off."

"Grace," her Father said, "you know that's not the way we do things in heaven or on the earth."

Grace knew why God wasn't pleased. She wasn't stupid or uninformed. She had memorized the Creator's rules against physical or spiritual violence but she had never understood how difficult it was to live by the principles of nonviolence especially on the field of battle.

Grace wanted to follow God's way, but not if it meant giving Demion a second chance. If he had come to cause more suffering for God's Queer Children the kind of suffering that breaks the loving heart of her Creator, why shouldn't she break the devil's scaly little neck instead and end the conflict then and there?

"Grace?" This time the voice had changed. It floated gently to the earth from that light in the room at the top of the tower.

"Yes, Mother," the tough little angel replied, recognizing God's other voice immediately but still refusing to set Demion free.

"You cannot conquer evil with evil," said the Mother of all Creation. "You can only conquer evil with good."

Grace had heard that gratuitous little paradigm at least a thousand times. She remembered writing it over and over on the blackboard after class. She wanted to please her Creator, but she wanted almost as much to squeeze the life out of that nasty, little devil. And have no doubt, she could do it.

"Grace?" This time God's voice seemed tired and far away.

"Yes," Grace answered.

"What did you hear God shout from heaven?"

For a moment, Grace didn't answer. Then she remembered that day when God appointed her a Guardian as they were looking over the edge of heaven listening to those ugly sounds echoing from the earth below. She was trying to recall the very words God had shouted. Then she remembered.

"I think the Father said, 'I love my Queer Children,'" Grace whispered. "I think that's all God said."

"Isn't that enough?" the voice asked quietly. "Your task is not to destroy the liars but to show the victims of those lies how much God loves them."

Convinced by the loving voice of God, Grace loosened her grip on Demion and set him free.

The angry soul thief fresh from hell scrambled out from under her, untangling his wings, shaking off the leaves and dirt, bouncing up and down on his hooves, jabbing left and right in her direction, glaring at her with his bright red eyes and threatening her with a whole repertoire of his most terrifying faces and foul four-letter words.

For a moment, Grace just stood there, hands at her side, looking up at him, scowling. Then suddenly, she saw him for what he really was. Demion was not her enemy. He was just another victim of the Evil One. Like all the others he had been taught to lie. It was the lie she fought, not the little devil who repeated it. At that moment she felt pity for this pitiful creature. Without thinking, Grace picked up his funny little pitchfork and handed it to him with a smile.

Demion had just met his match but already he hated her. The soul thief was at least a foot taller and twice her build yet she had won their first battle. Grace had humiliated him this time, but there were ways of getting even. Satan had given him good advice. Grace was limited by the Creator's love but hate has no limits.

"You will regret this moment," Demion growled at Grace, but it wasn't the little devil's voice she heard. It was the voice of Satan himself and she trembled at the sound.

"Fear not, Grace," Abba said quietly in response. "I am with you always even unto the end of the world."

Overhearing God's promise, Demion howled with rage and the hills around our campsite echoed with the sound.

I thought it was a California coyote howling the moon and I was afraid his lonely cry would awaken my tent mate, Jonathan. At the sound, he stirred, rolled over on his back and continued dreaming. I don't think I slept at all that night. Just looking at Johnny excited me. I wanted to touch his face, to kiss his cheek, to crawl into his sleeping bag and hold him in my arms. I was just thirteen. I didn't want to feel that way. I didn't want my body to react on its own without my permission. But every time I was around Johnny my body had reacted on its own and often at the worst possible times.

Earlier that evening after a visit to Mission Santa Cruz our "tribe" had put on leather loin cloths, moccasins made from scraps of leather and Indian headdresses shaped from feathers, straps and beads. Johnny had been chosen chief, the most brave and powerful. He wore an elaborate feathered war bonnet from our Scoutmaster's collection. The rest of us wore a feather for each merit badge we had won. Before our Native American guest could teach us the war dance, we were required to paint our tent mate's face, arms and chest with brightly colored war paint.

I panicked. For my fellow Scouts it was just a weird exercise in painting circles, lines and dots with bare fingers on boy's bare bodies. For me, it was torture. Facing Johnny, wearing only a loin cloth, finger painting his chest, our bodies almost naked, I could feel it happening again and this time there was no way for me to cover my shame. I tried to hide, to back into the shadows. I thought no one would see me there but Johnny noticed and walked in my direction. As the other boys in our tribe locked arms around the campfire and prepared to dance he grabbed my hand and pulled me into the circle. The drums began to beat. The boys began to chant, to move slowly around the fire. Without saying anything Johnny took my arm and led me in the dance. Sixty years later I still remember that moment and the mixed feelings I had of absolute joy and absolute shame.

Later that night Johnny just rolled over on his side and went to sleep as though nothing had happened, as though nothing had changed. But I lay there beside him in a state of shock. Once again my body reacted to the moment on its own. Once again I was embarrassed and confused by what I was feeling. Why was I attracted to a boy when all the others talked about their girlfriends? Why did my body embarrass me by reacting on its own at times and in places there was no way to hide? Why was I different? I think it was that summer night in the woods above Santa Cruz that I began to hate my body and for the next thirty years I lived with my secret shame, praying that God would change me, wondering why God didn't answer my prayer.

No wonder I was wide awake when the coyote howled. I was certain that I would spot it in the moonlight but when I stepped out of my tent the howling stopped. Years later I learned it wasn't the howling of a coyote. It was a war cry. I had stepped into the middle of a battle field where my guardian angel, Grace, was defending me against a nasty little soul thief named Demion.

I wish I could have seen him that first morning, standing in the shadows, licking his wounds, hating Grace and plotting to steal my soul. I wish even more that I could have seen my guardian angel pin him to the ground and hold him there. I wish I could have heard the voices of Grace and Demion, the voices of good and evil as they fought over my soul. Then again, maybe I did hear them.

In fact, what happened on that misty, mountain morning so long ago was the beginning of a dream-like dialogue between the three of us that would continue for a lifetime. Our little talks have become for me another way of praying, a kind of conversational prayer.

First, I imagine Demion in the room and listen to what he has to say. Then in the same way I hear Grace respond. Sometimes I question each in turn. Now and then the solution is simple and appears quickly. Other times the three of us debate for hours, even days. One thing is certain. I've learned that I can't trust Demion. Evil always lies. But I can trust Grace.

I wish I could slip into my thirteen-year-old body and lie beside Johnny once again. Instead of staying awake all night troubled by questions without answers, I would have invited Demion and Grace to sit beside me on my sleeping bag.

Demion, the face of evil in my life, would have spoken first. I imagine him to represent that side of me that hates the light and loves the shadows. He's the naysayer, the pessimist, the greedy, selfish, violent little creep inside my brain. He's the moody, easily depressed, spoiled child in me that wants what I want when I want it and will whine and pout and stamp my feet until I get it.

I imagine Grace to represent the face of love. When she speaks even Demion has to listen because he knows that Grace has developed much more power than the right hook that knocked him to the ground and the painful hammer-lock that kept him there. Grace learned that real power is not based on physical force but on soul force, the kind of power that comes through the commitment to truth, love and justice.

In my mind, Grace speaks for that person the Creator hopes I'll become, the person I want to be who is patient and kind; who doesn't envy or boast; who is not puffed up with pride; who doesn't dishonor others; who is not self-seeking, not easily angered; who keeps no record of wrongs; who doesn't delight in evil but rejoices in the truth. That person always protects, always trusts, always hopes and always perseveres.

I'm sure you know that I didn't create that rather formidable list. Those goals are found in a love letter from the Apostle Paul. Needless to say, I'm not there yet (and that, my friend, is the understatement of the century).

Picture the three of us sitting on my sleeping bag looking at the beautiful young man sleeping beside me. Demion might say, "I know what you're thinking right now and it is sick and sinful. Shame on you!" Grace would respond quickly. "Wanting to touch your tent mate, to kiss him, to hold him in your arms is not sick or sinful. Those feelings are natural and right and wonderful."

Demion might have giggled or groaned or been disgusted when he saw how my body was reacting. But he would shut up and back off with one quick glaring glance from Grace who would then explain, "Those powerful sensual feelings you're having are a gift from your Creator. They will give you great joy and pleasure. God wants you to enjoy them."

Demion's sarcastic and judgmental retort would be, "But your tent mate is a boy. You have a crush on a boy. You're a homo, a faggot, a fairy." I can picture Grace biting her tongue and flexing her fist wanting desperately to be nonviolent but wanting even more to crack the little devil's skull.

After pulling herself together Grace would speak with a voice so serious it would make me shiver. "What I'm about to say you must never, never forget! Your life depends on it. Will you promise to remember?" I would nod wondering what could be so important.

"God has created you Gay," Grace would begin, "and whatever names idiots like Demion might call you, God loves you exactly as you were created. Forget what they say. Remember this! You are a child of God. You are not a mistake. You were created Gay and have a unique role to play in the life of your family, your church, your school, your society. Do not let the nasty, jealous, stupid ones confuse you with their labels from hell. You are Gay. Be proud and be grateful."

Demion would probably laugh out loud and then speak with his most sarcastic voice. "Be Gay," he would echo. "Be proud," he would mock. "Be grateful," he would taunt. And then lowering his voice until it sounded like the voice of Satan himself he would add. "And be alone and lonely for the rest of your life."

Demion knew how lonely I felt, how miserable my secret made me feel. He knew I wanted to be like the other boys, to have a girlfriend, to have someone I could love and who would love me in the same way. But Grace also knew what I was feeling. She would respond with truth to Demion's nasty lie.

"Just hang on for a while," she would say and her voice would be gentle, understanding. "One day and maybe one day soon you will find a boy who has the same feelings about you that you have about him. Until then you will discover that there are millions of God's Queer Children just like you who are not lonely, who are living wonderful, ful-filling lives; and even if you never find a long term partner or husband, you will find a community of friends, Gay and Straight alike, who will love you and understand you and bring great joy to your life."

If only I had imagined Grace and Demion that night at Scout camp. Handling my first infatuation would still have been awkward but now at last I know what was happening as I lay on my sleeping bag or danced around the fire. I was realizing that I was Gay, that I had been created differently from the norm, and that the difference was good and right and natural. I'm sorry I didn't know it then. I'm sorry there are so many people who still don't know it. It was Demion who deceived me. It is evil who continues to deceive millions of LGBTQ people by repeating his lie, "God can't really love you until you change." I believed him when I was thirteen. I don't believe him now. It took me far too long to realize that Demion can never be trusted, that evil always lies.

After re-living that night at camp, I would be glad to slip back into my seventy-seven-year-old body. As Grace had promised me, over the years my sexual orientation has been a source of so much joy and pleasure. Sex is still an important bond between Gary and me. Once he was young and sexy. Now he's a sexy old man but the desper-ate need for same-sex intimacy that first brought us together has been replaced by a different kind of love that has grown more and more stable and rewarding over the years.

When we began our relationship there was no way for me to know in advance the important qualities he has that would keep us together long after sex had lost its power. Now I love him for his faithfulness,

for his willingness to forgive and even forget, for his careful management of our rather limited resources, for not complaining (at least
not very often) that I give away so much money. I couldn't know those
special talents until years after our first kiss. It took a long time to
discover his skills at turning an empty house into a comfortable and
attractive home, an empty piece of dirt (no matter how small) into a
garden that brightens up the neighborhood, an almost empty fridge
into a half-way decent meal, and a secret savings account that he hid
in his sock drawer until we needed a vacation I thought we couldn't
afford.

However, I have to confess that even after all these years, Demion, the soul thief, still lurks nearby in the shadows of my mind. I
have learned too many times that evil has a way of sticking around.
Even at my age, Demion can tell a pretty convincing lie. And worse, I
have to confess that sometimes I believe him.

To make my decisions even more difficult, Demion has changed.
Evil is all grown up now, calm, shrewd and sophisticated. He pawned
his pitchfork to buy a Rolex. He covered his scaly red skin with Armani suits and Burberry slacks. Somehow he's managed to fit his sharp
little hooves into Tom Ford high top shoes hand-crafted in Italy. I
don't know what he's done with his tail. It's probably rolled up and
held in place by a gold clip from Tiffany's.

Demion has also changed his strategy. He no longer yells at me.
He learned that I am turned off by sarcasm. Now he pretends to love
me, that he cares about my soul, that he has no desire to steal it. He
winks and nods and beckons. He speaks softly with an underlying tone
of excitement and urgency. Sometimes no matter how hard I resist,
I stop to listen.

Fortunately when I weaken, when I allow Demion to lead me
astray, I know that Grace is always there to say again: "God loves you.
There is nothing you can think or say or do that could ever stop God
from loving you. And if you ever think for a moment that God has giv-
en up on you, just remember that is one of evil's most pernicious lies.

There are times that Grace and I have won great victories. Other
times, well, not so much. Whatever happens, she never stops remind-
ing me that my sexual orientation is a gift from God. Unfortunately
Demion never stops trying to trick me into wasting my gift, into misusing or exploiting it for my pleasure at another person's expense.

I wish I could blame the little devil for the mistakes I make. I can't. He doesn't even exist except in my imagination. There's no legitimate way to blame Demion or Satan or the forces of hell for my thoughts, words or actions that are evil and break the heart of my Creator. They are my responsibility and mine alone.

Here's the secret. Somewhere along the way I learned that in my weakest moments Grace is sufficient to see me through whatever evil comes my way. Grace is the voice of my Creator and when I'm smart enough to listen, her words are always the same: "God loves you! God forgives you. Now get off your butt and make us proud."

Sixty years have passed. We've all three aged a little. Demion's eyes are not so red, his face not quite so fearsome. Grace had hair that matched the color of her freckles but it's turning gray now. My once tan "beach boy" skin is pale and wrinkled and spotted with age. I've learned a lot from these sixty years with Grace and Demion. I have to admit that there are days when I wonder if I need Grace anymore. There are moments when I feel like I've outgrown her, that I can handle life on my own, that the evil I might do at my old age isn't all that evil. But every time I begin to think I could make it without Grace I see feathers floating softly to the ground from the sky just above my head.

Sometimes the feathers are the color of Demion's wings. Other times, the feathers come from Grace. Whenever I see those feathers being wafted about on the warm California air, I am reminded that the war for my soul continues. I will always need Grace because Demion, no matter how old and tired he becomes, is still out there determined to steal my soul. Next time you see feathers floating softly to the ground from the sky above your head, think of the little soul thief who was given your name and be thankful for God's Grace in your life.

Amen

Acknowledgments

Special Thanks to

Peter Drake, Executive Director, Coil Foundation
(coilfoundation.org)
For your Coil Foundation Writer's Grant, thank you, Peter,
for caring so much about victims of biblical intolerance.

David Kerley, Artist and Designer
Thank you for the cover, layout, and overall design
of **Grace and Demion.**

Toby Johnson and David Kerley, Editors
Thank you both for your skill, your patience and your tireless sense of humor.

Toby Johnson, Production Manager
2017 Edition of **Grace and Demion**

Andrew Wilds, Photographer
(awildsphotography@mac.com)
Thank you for the photographs used in **Grace and Demion.**

Charles Hefling, Illustrator
Thank you for your creative cover and "Confession" illustrations.

And thanks to all those first pre-publication readers for their encouraging
and helpful feedback,
especially Diana Westbrook, Bill Carpenter, and Peggy Campolo.

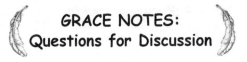

GRACE NOTES:
Questions for Discussion

Introduction

How would you define biblical intolerance?

Have you or anyone you know been a biblical intolerance victim?

Is the author correct when he writes: Well-meaning Christians still misuse the Bible to warn LGBTQ teenagers that their sexual orientation is from the devil and that accepting themselves as they are will send them straight to hell.

Chapter 1

Have you or anyone you know experienced "…years of guilt and self-hatred, endless 'ex-gay' therapy sessions, electric-shock and even exorcism" to "overcome" a "not acceptable" sexual orientation? (Consider reading the author's Stranger at the Gate: To Be Gay and Christian in America for his own personal experience of biblical intolerance and his 35 year struggle to overcome it.)

Chapter 2

Do you agree with the author that Gay is not a sufficient rainbow category to label everyone who is not heterosexual and that it would be awkward, if not impossible, to use LGBT (let alone LGBTQIA) as an inclusive label for non-heterosexuals in a book as long as Grace and Demion? Suggest another option?

Do you agree with the author's belief that "… eliminating that long string of letters helps disassociate us from the words society uses to divide us into sexual subgroups that caricature us, limit us and force us to be less than we are?"

Do you agree with the author that the word queer has been "claimed by the enemy" when in fact Queer can also mean "unique," "unconventional," and "set apart" and by reclaiming and redefining this word we transform an insult into a compliment and rob it of its power to hurt us?

Did you know that "Queer theology," "Queer studies," "Queer linguistics," etc. are the labels chosen by our own LGBTQ philosophers, historians, and theologians to describe their academic fields of study?

Did you know that the term transgender has been replaced by trans* to include all the diverse identities within the gender identity continuum (for example: transgender, transsexual, transvestite)?

Chapter 3

Are people born to hate or is hatred something passed on to us generation after generation? How is hate passed on to others? How is it possible to interrupt/stop the process of passing it on?

Chapter 4

What do you think the author is saying in these two exchanges between Grace and her Creator?

CREATOR: How could my Homofolk know that I love them when the air is filled with these condemning voices?"

GRACE: "Why don't you tell them yourself?"

CREATOR: "I have," God replied quietly, looking down across that long distance to the earth and remembering the prophets, the martyrs, the manger, cross, and empty tomb.

...

And in that sudden silence, God leaned out over space and said with a voice that all creation could hear, "I love my Queer Children!"

"Do you think they'll hear it?" Grace asked quietly.

"They will," God answered, "if they are listening."

Chapter 5

Why do these three words, "They are different," have the power to turn an entire village against two young men they have known from childhood. Have you ever been victimized by someone who sees you as "different"? Who do you find "different" in your own life?

What came to your mind when you read: "The lie must sound like Truth," the Prince of Lies told the Archdemon, "God's truth. It must sound like love," he added, "but it must lead to hate."

Chapter 6

How do you feel about St. Peter's remark: "In many tribes, in many lands, Transgender people have been called 'the two spirited ones.'..."Over the centuries," he said, "these 'two spirited ones' have often been chosen as spiritual leaders because they were seen to bridge the gap between male and female, to have been born with both spirits."

How did you feel when St. Peter told Grace: "All God's Children are special but God holds Transgender Children a little longer because they will need extra strength and courage down there where even their friends and family may not understand."

Chapter 7

What does Satan mean when he says: "Calling the Queer ones 'fruit' or 'faggot' or 'fairy' is a shortcut for saying 'God doesn't love you as you are?'"

Do you agree with Satan when he says: "It's even worse than calling their homo children 'dykes' or 'faggots' when parents say such things as: "You're such a disappointment..." or "We need to find someone who can help you..." or "You'll grow out of this..." or "Please don't tell your father..." Those "harmless little announcements are in fact a perfect way to disguise the lie that God doesn't love them as they are?"

What does Satan mean by his banquet toast: "To the really great lies and to the poor, dear liars who tell them believing sincerely that they are working for God when in fact, THEY ARE WORKING FOR US!"

Chapter 8

How do you respond to this dialogue between Moses and Paul?

MOSES: "Religious leaders have misused my words for centuries to prove that women are inferior; to stone women caught in the act of adultery; and to favor the children of Sarah while they wage war against Hagar's offspring."

PAUL: "And they've misused my words to drive lepers from our cities, to burn so-called witches and to keep women silent in the church."

MOSES: "Now, out of fear and ignorance they are misusing our words to condemn God's beloved Queer Children. As a result they are rejected at home, driven from their synagogues and churches, humiliated in the streets, tried unfairly, imprisoned, castrated, hanged, beheaded, and burned at the stake."

Do you agree with Paul when he claims that the story of Sodom is not about God's Queer Children: "Those who call God's Queer Children sodomites are sodomites themselves," Paul said. "When they close the doors of their homes or churches and make outcasts of God's Queer Children, they too are breaking God's heart and risking the wrath of heaven."

Chapter 9

What do you think Satan means when he says these words on the tour through Hell's Basement?"

"Our human friends don't need help when it comes to devising new ways to do evil, let alone torture God's Queer Children. But as a kind of favor to them, I take all the credit down here for what they do on their own up there."

Do you agree with Satan when he explains the power of his lie?

"To whisper 'they are different' has the power to wreck a family or launch a world war. Hitler and his goose-stepping stooges whispered 'they are different' and millions of Jews and other innocent people including God's Queer ones were murdered in ways so hideous that even I was surprised at human ingenuity."

True or false? "It is a lie to say that God's Queer Children need to be cured."

True or false? "That lie is the primary reasons God's Queer Children suffer and die."

Chapter 10

How do you explain St. Peter's description of the Light "at the right hand of God?"

"He is Truth and Love and Justice ... It is the Son."

"Whenever I see the light I remember an old friend and how brightly the Light shined in him and how in spite of my failures he caused the Light to shine in me."

Recall Peter's experience of failure and forgiveness. Is your story similar in any way?

How do you feel about the way Sister Teresa and Princess Diana answer Grace's question, "What should I do when I find one of God's Queer Children suffering and dying alone?" "Just reach out and touch them," Diana answers. "Just touch them," Teresa adds, "and God will do the rest?

NOTE: On August 31, 1997, Princess Diana was killed in an auto accident. Five days later, September 5, 1997, Sister Teresa died of cardiac arrest.

Chapter 11

How did you feel when you first read these words by Satan:

"People must never learn that misusing their Holy Book to support evil began as one of my best ideas. Now misusing it has become a Christian tradition, especially by those who take it literally."

What does it mean to say "You can take the Bible literally or you can take the Bible seriously? You can't do both." Do you agree?

When Satan tells Demion to misuse the Bible to condemn God's Queerfolk he adds, "There are just six or seven brief verses that you can use to clobber God's queer ones. You don't have to read the rest of it. Just memorize those six or seven verses and every time a queer comes up for air, have his or her friends and family misuse those ugly little lines again."

NOTE: If you are not familiar with the 6-7 Clobber Passages, consider downloading a copy of the author's What the Bible Says – and Doesn't Say – about Homosexuality at www.melwhite.org and www.soulforce.org

Discuss Satan's list of modern historical, psychological and scientific facts that must be ignored before the Bible can be misused to condemn God's Queerfolk. (pages 59-60) Do you agree?

Discuss Satan's list of atrocities committed by those who use the Bible literally. (page 60)

How do you respond to Satan's description of living the "closeted" life?

"If God's Queer Children hear those passages often enough they will begin to believe them. They will retreat deep into their closets, exactly where we want them, in the dark, alone, cut off from families and friends, isolated by guilt, traumatized by fear, dying to love and be loved, feeling lost, angry and without hope, convinced that even God doesn't love them."

After Satan describes what can happen in a closet to God's Queer Folk, Demion adds, "Those closets sound like hell to me?"

Does your own personal story, or the story of someone you know, illustrate the terrible consequences of living in a "closet"? Are there times when it is necessary and wise to keep one's sexual orientation secret? Is there a way to keep that secret from those who would hurt or abandon you and at the same time come out (of the closet) to close trustworthy friends and family?

Chapter 12

How did you feel when Grace hears these words in the Tower: " I am your Mother, Grace, as I am your Father. I have created you and I love you just as you are." Are you offended when you hear God described as Mother or addressed as "She?"

See these biblical passages for examples of God as mother:

- Hosea 13:8 God described as a mother bear;
- Deuteronomy 32:11-12 God described as a mother eagle;
- Deuteronomy 32:18 God who gives birth;
- Isaiah 42:14) God as a woman in labor;
- Matthew 23:37 and Luke 13:34 God as a Mother Hen.

Why do you think the author insists that it is important for God's Queerfolk to hear these words over and over again, "I love you, child. I love you exactly as you are?"

Chapter 13

Does your story or the story of someone you know illustrate the truth in these words by Satan?

"Never forget, when you maim the soul of the boy, you maim the soul of the man."

Is Satan exaggerating when he makes the following claims?

"If you really want to steal the souls of God's Queer Children," Satan said quietly, "you don't have to misquote their holy book. You can trust their pastors, priests and Sunday school teachers to misuse those seven little verses against them. You don't have to call them 'faggots,' or 'fairies,' or 'dykes.' Their classmates and co-workers will do that for you. You don't have to make them feel condemned or abandoned or unloved. Their parents and friends are experts in that department. And you don't even have to lie about them, or whip up the nation into a violent, homophobic frenzy, or organize voters to eliminate their civil rights. I have special friends up there who are doing all that very effectively. But to steal the souls of God's queer ones, there is one thing you must do without fail....To steal the souls of God's beloved Queer Children, you must make them believe they ought to change."

Do you have examples of family, friends, pastors, priests, teachers, politicians and activists whose lives are dedicated to ending biblical intolerance? Share stories of those who are working to establish full equality for LGBTQ people.

Have there been moments of guilt and shame in your life (or in the life of someone you know) that are similar to the author's experiences as a thirteen year old Boy Scout infatuated with his tent mate, Johnny?

When Grace has Demion pinned to the ground ready to "...finish him off" the Mother of all Creation says: "You cannot conquer evil with evil. You can only conquer evil with good." How do you feel about the author's call to follow the principles of nonviolent resistance in a world where heavily armed students are killing other students and nations are using weapons of mass destruction to wage war against their neighbor?

Note: The author and his partner, Gary Nixon, are the co-founders of Soulforce, an organization committed to ending religion-based oppression through the principles of nonviolent resistance. For more about nonviolence see www.soulforce.org and/or www.melwhite.org.

Why do you think Grace insists that the young gay man "...never, never forget" these words:

"God has created you Gay and whatever names idiots like Demion might call you, God loves you exactly as you were created. Forget what they say. Remember this! You are a child of God. You are not a mistake. You were created Gay and have a unique role to play in the life of your family, your church, your school, your society. Do not let the nasty, jealous, stupid ones confuse you with their labels from hell. You are Gay. Be proud and be grateful."

Whether you are LGBTQ or Straight, do you agree with the advice given? Have you experienced the results of those beliefs in your life? Do you agree with Grace in the above quote?

What point do you think the author is making when he describes Evil's new look?

"To make my decisions even more difficult, Demion has changed. Evil is all grown up now, calm, shrewd and sophisticated. He pawned his pitchfork to buy a Rolex. He covered his scaly red skin with Armani suits and Burberry slacks. Somehow he's managed to fit his sharp little hooves into Tom Ford high top shoes hand-crafted in Italy. I don't know what he's done with his tail. It's probably rolled up and held in place by a gold clip from Tiffany's."

Grace is the guardian angel's name but grace is also a key to understanding the Christian faith. How do you see (or how have you seen) grace at work in your life?

Do you agree with this statement?

"Here's the secret. Somewhere along the way I learned that in my weakest moments Grace is sufficient to see me through whatever evil comes my way. Grace is the voice of my Creator and when I'm smart enough to listen, her words are always the same: 'God loves you! God forgives you. Now get off your butt and make us proud.'"

The author has partially disguised references to positive/powerful Bible verses throughout his fable. Here are two he uses in this final chapter. Read the verses from their biblical source and share your honest feelings about them:

"Fear not, Grace," Abba said quietly. "I am with you always even unto the end of the world." (Matthew 28:20)

> *"I have learned in my weakest moment that Grace is sufficient to see me through."*
>
>   (II Corinthians 12:9)

What moments from Grace and Demion do you remember most vividly? How did it affect you?

Is there something about Grace and Demion you found unhelpful even damaging to your own spiritual journey?

To whom would you recommend Grace and Demion? Why?

The Rev. Dr. Mel White

Winner of the ACLU'S National Civil Liberties Award, the Rev. Dr. Mel White has served the Christian community for thirty years as a pastor, professor, author, filmmaker, and ghost writer to some of the nation's most powerful religious figures. After a thirty year struggle to "overcome his homosexuality" through various "therapies" from exorcism to electric shock, Dr. White finally accepted his sexual orientation as "a gift from God." With Gary Nixon, his partner (husband) of thirty-seven years, he co-founded Soulforce, a network of volunteers across the U.S. using the tools of nonviolence to help end religion based oppression.

In his autobiography, **Stranger at the Gate: To Be Gay and Christian in America**, Dr. White chronicles "coming out" of his closet to bring hope and healing to his LGBTQ sisters and brothers and to begin his own justice ministry on their behalf. In his second book, **Holy Terror: Lies the Christian Right Tells Us to Deny Gay Equality**, he reveals the frightening plan of fundamentalist Christians to reconstruct American democracy into a theocracy. Dr. White was a member of the Organizing Committee of the National Council of Elders, "Leaders of 20th century civil rights and justice movements organizing to support similar nonviolent movements of the 21st Century."

Dr. White's daughter, Erinn Rich, is a second grade teacher and the mother of his grandchildren Katie and Sean. His son-in-law, Dr. Terry Rich is a chiropractor. His son Mike is a filmmaker ("Dawson's Creek," "School of Rock," "Nacho Libre"). Dr. White and Mike were a popular team on seasons 14 and 18 of the Amazing Race (CBS).

To Gary Nixon

for thirty-seven years

Lover, Partner, Husband, Friend

On your 50th birthday and for thirteen birthdays since, I have written a chapter of Grace and Demion just for you. Now we've shared our little secret with the world. There will be people who don't like our fable. That's OK. It's rather obvious that I'm no C.S. Lewis. But I'm hoping that the Spirit of Truth will use this simple story to bring hope and healing to our sisters and brothers who are victims of biblical intolerance and abuse as we have been. Whatever good it does in their lives would not have happened without you!

Md

Happy Birthday

For up to date information on the adventures of
the Guardian Angel and the Soul Thief,
visit the author's webpage:

www.melwhite.org

To purchase multiple copies of **Grace and Demion**
at reduced rates, please contact:

Dr. White at
GraceandDemion@gmail.com

Endorsements Continued...

A stirring fable and a paradigm-shifting look at what it means to be a 'sodomite.' The Majesty doesn't care who we love but we can't spurn a stranger without becoming sons & daughters of Sodom.

Jay Jarman, Pastor, church planner, children's advocate in Hawaii

A fresh and innovative story.

Matthew Carnicelli, Carnicelli Literary Management

A warm, moving, simple story. A fable that carries profound truth in its delivery. And though they are totally different, it has a place alongside Dr. White's **Stranger at the Gate**.

Mike Herrington, Gay activist

Took me back through my own sadness, grief, loneliness and finally jubilation for being true to myself. **Grace and Demion** will touch everyone who has gone through any persecution about their sexuality.

Nelson Rojas, educator, Corona del Mar High School

An absolutely brilliant concept to illuminate the corners of darkness in people's minds! I was blown away by it. What a source of comfort and help it will be in counseling LGBTs or their families. I found it mind expanding!

Harold Kameya, founder Asian Pacific Islander PFLAG

Inspired, delightful and profound! This splendid fable speaks the truth, with both force and tenderness, about God's unconditional love and the inherent dignity and integrity of lesbian, gay, bisexual and transgender people.

Jimmy Creech, pastor defrocked by the UMC for performing a same-gender wedding

Grace and Demion offers healing, hope and freedom to all of us who were taught in our childhood that we are sick and sinful. Helps us remember the painful challenges and re-claim our power as whole and healthy queer people! Thank you Mel!

Bill Carpenter, long-time activist and supporter

Grace & Demion is down to earth, yet communicates heavenly truth uniquely as only a beautifully structured fable can. I am convinced that one day it will be regarded a classic for intertwining in unique fashion a subtle theology of reconciliation with earthly encouragement that helps LGBT people better navigate this tumultuous and difficult life."

Dr. Calvin R. Schoonhoven, professor

I no longer believe in the Christian religion. It has hurt too many innocent people, including my daughter, Anna and myself. That's why **Grace and Demion** is important. It uses humor to undermine the threat of hell that Christian's use to keep LGBTQ people in their closets feeling guilty and afraid. And I'm glad for that.

Mary Lou Wallner, Co-founder (with husband Bob), Teach-Ministries

Being the mother of a gay son, I would have given any amount of money to have had a book like this to share with him when he first told me. This story is told with such simple understanding but also with such wisdom only God can grant.

Faith Delk, proud mother of a gay son, local organizer

For us — the parents of homofolk — Mel White takes up where C.S. Lewis left off, giving us a bridge to God after all of ours built earlier in life lay in ruin.

G. Kenneth West, Ph.D., professor of counseling and human development,

This fable is not just about LGBTQ people. It's about humanity. It's about God who never stops loving us. I'm a gay Jewish man, but I would recommend it to anyone seeking a gorgeous jolt of hope, inspiration and true wisdom.

Ken Page, LCSW, author, **Finding Love and Deeper Dating**

My Bible quoting Father didn't know that his son was busy building interior walls that hid my need to be a girl. How vastly more productive, loving, and happy my life could have flowed had I known that

God created me exactly as I am … and that God had held me close a moment longer because the path to wholeness is difficult.

Judy Osborne, long-time Transgender activist

I love it. So much truth spun in a very thought provoking and yet entertaining style. This will minister to the many harmed by Biblical intolerance and to those seeking with open hearts to understand what is happening to themselves and to those they love.

Jane Clementi, co-founder, the Tyler Clementi Foundation

Grace and Demion is so wonderful that I don't have adequate words to describe it. I know I want at least 20 copies to give as gifts to special friends who badly need your words. For the first time in my life, I was not offended by the word "Queer." And I have been offended by it for a long time, ever since I first heard it. Your story changed my mind.

Peggy Campolo, activist, lay counselor and public speaker

An appealing, unconventional adult fable that uses a comic style for a serious purpose: The story is a moving allegory for Mel's own life and his brave struggle to free himself and other LGBT people from religious oppression.

Kittredge Cherry, author, **Equal Rites** and founder of JesusInLove.org

A brilliant way to find a more compassionate place for self and others through fantasy characters, rather than having to actually look at reality. The Guardian Angels visit to the city of Sodom sheds such a great light on the true sin of its people.

Dr. Becky Kuhn, M.D., HIV/AIDS physician and educator

Grace and Demion combines the demon-in-training storytelling of **Screwtape Letters** with the real life suffering Satan's lies bring to LGBT. The triumphant news that The Creator loves the rich diversity of creation echoes through heaven and hell and will bring welcome news to many wounded Christians.

Rev. Julie Nemecek, long-time Transgender activist

Mel's God looks over the edge of Heaven and shouts to the earth, "I love my Queer Children!" Little angel Grace asks, "Do you think they'll hear it?" "They will," God answered, "if they are listening." If you are listening to what Mel writes in **Grace and Demion**, you will hear it too.

The Rev. Steve Kindle, E.D., Clergy United, author, **Marriage Equality,**

In his intensely autobiographical **Stranger at the Gate**, Mel White provided a compelling and eye-opening look at being gay and Christian and, perhaps most important, at the spirit-crushing challenges caused by churches and religious leaders with their misguided teachings about homosexuality. Now, with the imaginative fable of **Grace and Demion**, White imparts an important truth, that the "still small voice" those Christians purport to hear may not be from the Master they suppose.

Diana G. Westbrook, M.A., ABC, Soulforce leadership team, 99 – 05

Gay people are not given myths through traditional culture with which we can explain our experience to ourselves. We have to create our own myths. Stories like Mel White's Grace and Demion (which I had the good fortune to assist with editing) is a delightful and wise example of how to rearrange the old stories in order to create deeply meaningful, satisfying and revelatory personal myths.

Toby Johnson, author, **Gay Perspective** and **Gay Spirituality**

"So many of the at-risk queer youth and their families will never read a 'serious' book of theology. Our world needs serious theology, but it needs good news of unconditional love simply told far more. Mel White has made it plain! God loves the queer children God created. **Grace and Demion** offers life-saving and soul-saving good news for everyone."

The Rev. Harry Knox, Human Rights Campaign's Religion and Faith Program